Health starts in the kitchen, which is why I dedicate this book to each and every one of you who is taking the empowered decision to cook your way to being well and happy.

SMART CARBS

MAKE CARBS WORK FOR YOU AND UNLOCK
THE KEY TO WEIGHT LOSS AND GREAT HEALTH!

LUKE HINES

plum. Pan Macmillan Australia

CONTENTS

INTRODUCTION

I am so incredibly excited to be able to share with you in this book what I believe to be the easiest, most delicious way to eat for optimum health and happiness – an approach to food that leaves stress and feelings of restriction at the door, while celebrating all that is mouth-wateringly tasty and incredibly good for you too!

Now, I don't blame you if you're totally confused about what you should eat, how you should eat it, how much of it you can have and when is the best time to do so – particularly when it comes to carbohydrates. The world of healthy eating, fad diets and quick-fix solutions can get really confusing, especially when it changes as quickly as Melbourne's weather! The truth is, there is so much information and misinformation out there that most of us are left scratching our heads wondering how many carbs we should be eating per day, what sources they should come from … or even whether we should be eating them at all!

My aim with this book is to make looking and feeling your best as easy, enjoyable and delicious as possible, while providing you with a sustainable, long-term dietary approach that will reduce your cravings, boost your mood and have you feeling energised like never before! To do this I am going to introduce you to what I call 'The Smart Carb Curve', which I have designed to help you find an approach to healthy eating that works specifically for you as an individual, based on your health and lifestyle. It all comes down to a wonderful thing called bio-individuality – which I will also talk about shortly – and you're going to love it!

First, though, a quick recap of my food philosophy. Throughout my previous books I have shared recipes with you that celebrate real, nutrient-dense foods and avoid foods that may cause you harm and inflammation. Common inflammatories include gluten, dairy and refined sugars, so as a starting point, all of the recipes I create are automatically 100% free of these, giving you guys a really good health 'baseline'. This book is a safe zone for all those looking to remove or minimise these foods from their diet. The Smart Carbs focus is on finding the right balance between the most nutrient-dense foods to help us reach our individual health, wellness and happiness goals.

So how do you go about working out the right balance for you? Well, that's where you need to follow my Smart Carb Curve (see page 13) and get 'into the zone'. There are three main zones on my curve – the Keto Zone, the Low-Carb Zone and the Sustain Zone, with all of the recipes in this book suiting one (or more) of these zones. Each zone has its own approach to eating carbs and each will suit different people for different reasons – all you have to do is work out where you sit on the Smart Carb Curve, then opt for the corresponding recipes to deliver the level of carbs you need, together with supporting macronutrients in the form of healthy fats and quality proteins. Before you know it, you will find yourself well on your way to developing an individual, sustainable, long-term approach to healthy eating that never skimps on deliciousness.

Personally, I am thrilled to be able to delve into this space, which is so often the missing piece in our overall health puzzle. Looking closely at our carb consumption and resetting it to best benefit us as individuals allows us to take things to the next level, enabling us to work on fine-tuning specific things like reducing excess body fat and increasing energy levels, leaving us feeling happier and healthier overall. So, what are you waiting for? It's time to get started and learn more about how wonderfully unique we all are!

BIO-INDIVIDUALITY: IT'S ALL ABOUT YOU

Imagine being able to eat the most delicious foods on the planet – foods that leave you feeling satiated and energised to take on anything that life throws at you, foods that allow you to say goodbye to cravings and remove any of the stress or guilt you may have towards what you eat. Well, welcome to your unique bio-individuality!

As a personal trainer and nutritional therapy practitioner I have experienced first-hand the trials and tribulations people go through every day to achieve their health and wellness goals. All of us, myself included, strive to look and feel our best, but how do we go about doing so? What should we eat? How should we move, and what's the best way to manage life's stressors on top of all of this? Should we quit sugar? Or embark on a juice cleanse? Is dairy really bad for us?

There is so much noise and misinformation out there surrounding our diets and lifestyles that I wouldn't blame you for being confused and overwhelmed. But what's fact and what's fiction? Well, I have good news for you, which I hope will enable you to move forward, confidently and in the right direction, backing yourself, knowing that you're doing the right thing. Here goes …

There is no one-size-fits-all approach to diet and lifestyle.

There, I said it. Feels good, doesn't it? To know that, even with all that abundance of information out there – and with medicine and science constantly looking for that magic bullet – no one way of eating will work for everyone. And to know that, even if you haven't yet found exactly what you're looking for, it is possible to look and feel your best in all aspects of your life by listening to your body and working out the best way to nourish yourself from the inside out.

Each and every person has their own unique needs – it's working out what those needs are that will help you to thrive.

THE NUTRITIONAL BASICS

To make the most of the principles contained in this book, it's really important to understand the basics surrounding protein, carbohydrates and fats, and how we use these macronutrients as sources of energy to function optimally, fight disease and stay feeling happy and healthy. As this is a cookbook and not a school textbook, I will keep this light and brief but trust me, understanding these macronutrients is an important part of the puzzle in figuring out your own bio-individuality.

As humans, we have an incredible ability to conserve, expend and generate energy. But how do we know how much protein, carbohydrate and fat we need to eat as individuals to provide us with enough energy to maintain a healthy weight? This comes down to finding the right balance that suits us as individuals, and that means following five simple steps:

1. Understanding your individual energy needs
2. Evaluating your current health and long-term wellbeing goals
3. Choosing an appropriate carbohydrate zone to complement these factors
4. Celebrating the abundance of food choices on offer within your zone
5. Balancing your meals, mindset and moves for long-term, sustainable results

There is no 'one size fits all' approach to diet and lifestyle.

PROTEINS

Proteins are the main building blocks of the body. They do most of the work in our cells and are used to make muscles, tendons, organs and skin as well as the enzymes, hormones, neurotransmitters and various tiny molecules vital to our overall health and wellbeing. Made up of smaller units called amino acids, proteins are predominately found in animal meats but are also present in some plants, fruits, nuts, seeds, poultry, vegetables and dairy. But how much protein should we be eating?

The recommended daily intake of protein is a little under 1 gram per kilogram of body weight. Although this amount may be enough to prevent a deficiency, studies show that the 'right' amount of protein for any one individual depends on many factors, including activity levels, age, muscle mass, physique goals and current state of health (don't worry, we will get on to that soon).

If our body is satiated with the correct level of fats, protein will be efficiently and effectively used to promote the repair and rebuilding of cells. The aim is to eat enough protein to stay satiated and prevent muscle wastage without eating too much, as excess protein will convert to excess glucose.

CARBOHYDRATES

Carbohydrates are the sugars, starches and fibres found in fruits, grains, vegetables and milk products. While nowadays there is an increasing amount of concern surrounding them, carbs are still one of the basic food groups and – when eaten correctly – can be very important to our health. Together with protein and fat, they are one of the three main ways the body obtains energy.

If you're overweight or struggle with energy levels, it's likely that your carbohydrate metabolism is dysfunctional. You may be insulin resistant, so even moderate amounts of carbs will do a real number on you.

So how many carbs do we need? Typically, 100–150 grams of carbs per day is enough to keep us out of ketosis (more on this later) but not so much that we start to store the excess as fat. If you are looking to lose excess body fat, keeping carbs under 100 grams a day will help to lower insulin levels and tap into stored fat supplies for energy. But if your fitness goals or lifestyle have you training hard for long periods of time, you might have a larger window for carbohydrate intake. Again, it is always going to come down to what your individual body needs based on your lifestyle and level of movement. To work out the best approach for you, read on!

FATS

You might be wondering where, if you eat a moderate amount of protein, combined with a lower-carb approach, you'll be getting your fuel from. The answer is simple – fat! I really hope you learn to love the stuff, because if I were to list all the benefits of getting good fats into your diet I could fill this whole book …

Fat is essential to human life – the key is working out how much of it is right for each of us. It enables our bodies to process vitamins A, D, E and K, which are vital to good health, while some fatty acids like omega-3 may provide other health benefits such as complementing the cognitive processes of the brain and reducing inflammation. Fat has little to no impact on our insulin levels and as a result promotes the burning of consumed fat as fuel, as well as helping us tap into the body's fat stores for use as fuel. And as fat is such a concentrated source of energy, we often find that when we eat good fat we need less food to feel satiated, meaning we are less likely to overeat. Plus it makes food taste better! What's not to love?

So, regardless of how many carbs you need, I suggest that fat becomes your major fuel source. Find the right balance of protein and carbs you need each day, stay fairly consistent and you can then use fat as the major energy variable in your diet. So, if you're feeling hungry, rather than becoming a slave to sugar cravings (and the associated slumps in energy) reach for some good fat! The recipes in this book contain incredible sources of good fats that will keep you feeling fuller for longer, while also helping you to reach your health and wellness goals (for more on fats, see page 17). Consumed wisely, fats will help you feel full, stop you starving and have you looking and feeling great – what more can you ask for?

THE KEYS TO UNDERSTANDING YOUR ENERGY NEEDS

Whether you are looking to undertake a diet or lifestyle change, or simply looking to fine-tune where your health is at, you should bear in mind the following four important principles for optimal functioning in relation to your energy needs:

1. LOOK TO MINIMISE EXCESS BODY FAT Studies show that holding on to excess body fat can increase your risk of disease, making it harder for you to maintain your health and happiness.

2. FOCUS ON INCREASING LEAN MUSCLE MASS Lean muscle mass is directly associated with longevity, immunity and vibrant health. So, rather than focusing on losing 'weight', focus instead on losing fat and increasing lean muscle mass.

3. REDUCE EXCESS INSULIN Research in both animals and humans has shown that producing less insulin keeps us living longer and lighter, with high insulin levels linked to type-2 diabetes, obesity, heart disease and cancer. High insulin levels can also lead to insulin resistance, which can in turn result in producing more insulin, creating a vicious cycle.

4. NEVER FORGET THE 80/20 RULE Your body composition comes down to 80% diet and 20% exercise. So as important as it is to sweat it out and train, the vast majority of your results come from what, how and when you eat. If you truly want a health transformation, you need to learn to love the kitchen.

TO CARB OR NOT TO CARB?

It's really important to note that the 'c' word isn't a dirty word at all and there's no such thing as quitting carbs completely – the idea is impossible! Why? As we've already established, carbohydrates are one of the body's main macronutrients and key sources of energy – they are not the same thing as just pasta, rice, bread and baked goods, they are also in everything that is good for you including fruit and both starchy and non-starchy vegetables (and even whole dairy for those who choose to consume it). Yes, you can give up grains, sweets, breads and other starchy carbohydrates, but you can't really give up all carbohydrates. You can, however, look at finding the right balance of carbs in your diet to help you achieve your own individual health, wellness and happiness goals.

It can be very confusing trying to make sense of all the messages out there right now when it comes to carbohydrates, particularly as different people will be able to handle different amounts of carbohydrates in their diet. At one end of the scale, highly active individuals and athletes will have no problem handling a higher number of carbs, as their energy demands are higher than those of sedentary people, whereas at the other end diabetics will do a lot better on fewer carbs as they are unable to physiologically manage normal carbohydrate metabolism. But what about the rest of us? The everyday working, parenting, studying, hit the gym from time to time man or woman – are we eating too many? If you're noticing your belly grow a little bigger, find yourself suffering energy crashes and craving sweets all the time, or are suffering from hormonal or fatigue issues, the answer could be yes.

If you struggle with your weight in particular – either you're unable to lose it or find yourself gaining it as time goes on – then it's likely that you have some type of carbohydrate dysfunction. Insulin resistance is one of the most common issues people experience, and here is how it works. When we eat carbs, they are largely broken down into glucose, one of the body's main fuel sources. When the glucose is absorbed into the bloodstream, the pancreas releases insulin, which indicates to cells throughout the body that there is excess glucose for them to absorb and use. When we eat too many carbohydrates, the cells can become resistant to the insulin, but the pancreas keeps producing it because the blood glucose levels remain high. Because the cells haven't used the glucose in the blood, the body eventually converts it into fat for storage.

The good news is that there is a carb appropriate approach that will help you reset – return you to your natural body weight and deliver all the natural energy and vitality that comes with it. It's about resetting the balance and discovering what is right for you. And the even better news is, this book has you covered.

HOW DO I WORK OUT HOW MANY CARBS I SHOULD BE EATING?

Fantastic question … and you'll also want to work out the ratio you should be consuming your fats and proteins in while you are at it! It's about listening to your body and creating a baseline to measure against. My suggestion for working out what balance of these three macronutrients works best for you is to assess this over a longer period of time, and then, based on an average overall approach, make suitable adjustments, rather than sweating the small stuff.

So, rather than counting each and every meal down to the calories and macronutrients, focus on the bigger picture and make measured decisions – not rash, extreme changes that can result in an inability to follow a particular way of eating properly. We all experience feelings of disappointment when we fall off the health wagon, derailing our best intentions and lowering our motivation to stay on track. I therefore think it's far more effective to look at things over a much longer span of time, like a few weeks, and aim for an 'average' consumption of fantastic foods, gauge how we feel based on these levels and then adjust accordingly. It would simply be impossible to accurately gauge your exact daily meal-to-meal requirements, plus it would drive you bananas. If after a month or more you've been fairly consistent, you'll have an average of daily protein, fats and carbs to easily adjust.

When evaluating the results of a particular dietary approach, please don't just focus on weight loss or weight gain. How you feel is so much more important than numbers on a scale, especially when there are so many variables. I truly believe that if you can get your health and happiness under control, your body weight and fitness will fall into place. Later on I touch on Meals, Mindset and Moves (see page 22), and once you've found synergy between these three elements, so many pieces of the health puzzle will fall into place for you, giving you the reassurance and motivation to keep going forward positively.

Also, keep in mind that no-one is perfect and that life throws us curve balls, so make peace with the fact that you will, from time to time, eat terrible plane food, steal leftovers from the kids' lunchboxes or enjoy a piece of birthday cake. That's life. There will be weeks where you train like a machine and others where you watch every series your streaming service has to offer without leaving the couch. We need to keep looking at the big picture – that, as an average, we don't let our consumption of macronutrients fall out of balance, that we keep in mind where we are getting our fuel from and that we stay in the zone.

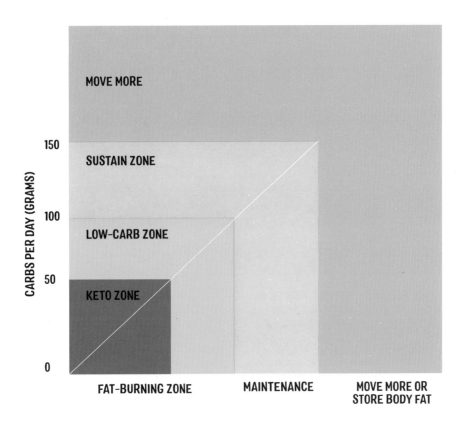

THE SMART CARB CURVE: HOW LOW SHOULD YOU GO?

Feeling and looking our best should be easy, which is why I want to introduce you to the Smart Carb Curve – an easy-to-understand guide to working out how low you should go carb-wise to support a happy and healthy lifestyle that suits you as an individual.

Take a look at the scale and you'll see it compares the amount of carbs consumed per day with your body's energy balance and efficiency in either burning more fat, maintaining your current body composition or increasing stored body fat if you don't live an active enough lifestyle. Let's take a closer look at what all of these mean, allowing you to make informed, sensible and most of all sustainable choices when it comes to delicious food.

THE KETO ZONE

0–50 grams of carbohydrate per day

This level of carbohydrate intake allows for easy, effortless weight loss for most people. It's important your fat intake is sufficient to support this very low-carb intake by supplying you with ketones (by-products of the breakdown of fatty acids) as your energy source.

It seems likely that our primal ancestors – those from prehistory – would have experienced periods of nutritional ketosis due to seasonal and environmental patterns, but would not have been in ketosis indefinitely or for prolonged periods of time. Therefore, while diabetics and the morbidly obese may find it useful to remain in this zone for extended periods, the average person might employ it now and then to jump-start weight loss or break a plateau before returning to the Low-Carb or Sustain zones.

THE LOW-CARB ZONE

50–100 grams of carbohydrate per day

This level of carbohydrate intake promotes steady, sustainable, gradual weight loss. This is the sweet spot for many and is certainly my favourite for people who want to enjoy a wide variety of foods while still losing excess body fat, maintaining lean muscle mass and feeling fantastic. Studies have shown this to be a more sustainable long-term approach than a very low-carb one for those of us who live normal, busy lives.

You'll struggle to eat more than 100 grams of carbohydrate a day if you follow a primal approach, eat colourful above-ground seasonal vegetables (even tonnes of them), avoid grains and processed and refined sugars, and eat your starchy below-ground vegetables and high-sugar fruits mindfully and in balance.

THE SUSTAIN ZONE

100–150 grams of carbohydrate per day

This is the perfect zone for you if you want to maintain your current body composition. For anyone new to this 'cleaner' approach to eating, I recommend this as your starting point – it's a smart and sustainable way to celebrate carbs from all the right sources without any feelings of restriction. You'll feel full and well balanced in terms of your energy levels, with fewer cravings and an increased sense of wellbeing.

Even if you eat a tonne of both above- and below-ground vegetables and a moderate amount of fruit, you'll be hard pressed to exceed 150 grams of carbs on average per day as the fats you consume as part of your diet will keep you feeling full and satiated, preventing overeating. Our primal ancestors wouldn't have been able to average 150 grams of carbs a day if they tried, yet they still had plenty of energy and maintained healthy lean muscle mass.

THE CARB EXCESS ZONE

150–300 grams of carbohydrate per day

This zone has been shown to promote steady weight gain. You know, the type that just creeps up on you when you are not very active and your physical wellbeing slows down at the same rate as your carb intake increases. This zone is a really common place for those of us who feel we're doing okay, but wondering why we can't lose weight (and instead find ourselves slowly putting it on). Unless you are an elite athlete with a very specific need for high carbohydrate levels, you don't need to consume this quantity of carbs.

THE WARNING ZONE

300+ grams of carbohydrate per day

Sadly, many people who follow an average approach to food and lack awareness of carb levels and the importance of moving their bodies fall into this zone. Unless you're an extreme endurance athlete, 300+ grams of carbs per day will inevitably show on your waistline. This is the zone where we can expect to see hormonal imbalances and fatigue issues, insulin resistance, type-2 diabetes and obesity.

FINDING THE RIGHT BALANCE

When reducing carbs at any level, it's important we find the right balance between our supplementary fats and proteins, as outlined in the charts on the opposite page. Regardless of which zone you sit in, you will see that healthy fat intake is paramount for optimal functioning, fat burning and energy.

Food is to be enjoyed, loved and celebrated, and finding the right balance between this and maintaining optimum health is really important. As a rough guide, if you're needing to lose excess body fat, the Keto or Low-Carb zones may suit you perfectly, whereas if you are looking to maintain your current health and wellbeing the Sustain Zone may be spot on for you (with some extra carbs added in for anyone exercising at an intense level if need be). It's also important to note that the Keto and Low-Carb recipes in this book can be enjoyed while following the Sustain approach, while Low-Carb and Sustain recipes can easily be adjusted to suit the Keto Zone (see page 28 for details).

MACRONUTRIENT BREAKDOWN PER CARB APPROACH

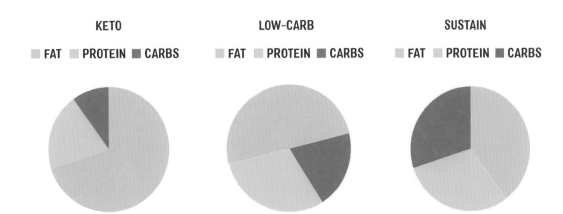

KETO
FAT   PROTEIN   CARBS

LOW-CARB
FAT   PROTEIN   CARBS

SUSTAIN
FAT   PROTEIN   CARBS

WHERE SHOULD WE BE GETTING OUR SMART CARBS FROM?

Carbohydrates come from a variety of sources and, depending on our health goals, some are better for us than others. Now, it's important to note again that, as per my overarching food philosophy, none of the recipes featured in this book include grains or legumes – meaning regular breads, rice, pasta and other similar starchy ingredients are off the menu (and that also goes for refined and processed foods, including sugary treats and lollies).

So which foods does that leave us with to stay on track in each zone? While there are some exceptions, as an overall rule, above-ground vegetables are a good source of carbs for those of us following a Keto or Low-Carb approach. Below-ground veg, on the other hand, are higher in starch, making them better for those following a Sustain approach. Fruit, nature's superfood, varies too – some lower-fructose options like berries and green apples pop up on the lower end of the carb zone, while other fruits such as bananas and mangoes are more suitable for those following a Sustain approach.

The chart overleaf on page 16 details where a variety of delicious, nutrient-dense real foods fit on the carb spectrum. You'll see that ingredients that fit within the Keto Zone can also be enjoyed by those in the Low-Carb and Sustain zones, while ingredients that are marked as Sustain are best avoided by those following a Keto or Low-Carb approach.

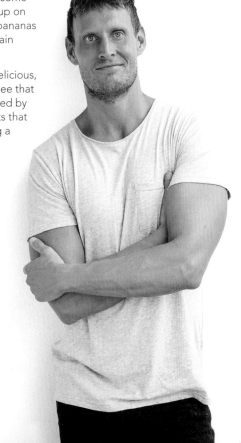

Your body composition comes down to 80% diet and 20% exercise. So as important as it is to sweat it out and train, the vast majority of your results come from what, how and when you eat.

INGREDIENT	ZONE(S)	INGREDIENT	ZONE(S)
artichoke	K, LC, S	radicchio	K, LC, S
asparagus	K, LC, S	radishes	K, LC, S
avocado	K, LC, S	raspberries	K, LC, S
bamboo shoots	K, LC, S	rocket	K, LC, S
bananas	S	spinach	K, LC, S
beetroot	LC, S	spring onion	K, LC, S
blackberries	K, LC, S	squash	K, LC, S
blueberries	K, LC, S	strawberries	K, LC, S
bok choy	K, LC, S	sweet potatoes	S
broccoli/broccolini	K, LC, S	tomatoes	K, LC, S
brussels sprouts	K, LC, S	turnips	K, LC, S
cabbage	K, LC, S	yams	S
capsicum	K, LC, S	zucchini	K, LC, S
carrots	S	beef	K, LC, S
cauliflower	K, LC, S	fish	K, LC, S
celery	K, LC, S	game	K, LC, S
chard	K, LC, S	lamb	K, LC, S
chicory greens	K, LC, S	pork	K, LC, S
chillies	K, LC, S	poultry	K, LC, S
citrus	K, LC, S	offal	K, LC, S
cucumber	K, LC, S	seafood	K, LC, S
daikon	K, LC, S	eggs	K, LC, S
dried herbs and spices	K, LC, S	nuts	K, LC, S
eggplant	K, LC, S	seeds	K, LC, S
endive	K, LC, S	shredded coconut	K, LC, S
fennel	K, LC, S	sauerkraut	K, LC, S
fresh herbs	K, LC, S	almond milk	K, LC, S
grapefruit	LC, S	coconut cream/milk	K, LC, S
kale	K, LC, S	coconut oil	K, LC, S
kohlrabi	K, LC, S	extra-virgin olive oil	K, LC, S
leeks	K, LC, S	grass-fed butter	K, LC, S
mixed lettuce	K, LC, S	coconut aminos	LC, S
mushrooms	K, LC, S	coconut sugar	S
okra	K, LC, S	dried berry powder	LC, S
olives	K, LC, S	grass-fed gelatine	K, LC, S
onions	K, LC, S	green leaf stevia	K, LC, S
palm hearts	K, LC, S	honey	S
parsnips	S	maple syrup	S
pears	LC, S	apple cider vinegar	K, LC, S
potatoes	S	mustard	K, LC, S
pumpkin	LC, S	sugar-free fish sauce	K, LC, S

OIL ME UP: UNDERSTANDING OILS AND FATS

Fat is an essential nutrient that is both good for us and makes food taste fantastic! Certain fats, like linoleic acid and alpha linoleic acid, are physiologically essential because your body simply cannot produce them by itself. Other fats, like those found in extra-virgin olive oil, grass-fed butter and coconut oil, are culinarily essential because they make food taste really good (while also being fantastic in the nutrition department).

Understanding which fats are good for you and which to avoid can make all the difference to succeeding long term with a healthy approach to looking after yourself. The table below is a great at-a-glance reference for the sort of foods containing good-quality fats that you should consume to balance your carbohydrate approach, regardless of which zone you fall into. So whether it's the oil you use for cooking, or the fats on your plate in each meal, here's my Terrific 21.

avocado oil	cacao butter	lard	avocados
coconut oil	coconut butter	tallow	eggs
extra-virgin olive oil	grass-fed butter	coconut milk and cream	nuts
macadamia oil	duck fat	fatty animal cuts	olives
MCT/ KETO oil	ghee	oily fish	seeds

CELEBRATING HEALTHY FATS

For years, saturated fats were seen as harmful for our health and we were advised to reduce our intake of them as much as possible (even now, many dietitians suggest doing this). The good news is that most recent studies have debunked this myth, showing no significant link between saturated fats – which humans have been eating for thousands of years – and the risk of heart disease, while also detailing the many healthy benefits of including these fats in our diet, which include:

- Boosting immune system health
- Supporting the creation of important hormones like cortisol and testosterone
- Maintaining bone density
- Raising HDL (good) cholesterol in the blood and lowering LDL (bad) cholesterol

I love healthy saturated fat as it can be digested easily and is a fantastic source of energy, ideal for when you want to increase your fat intake while reducing carbs. No matter which zone you target, following my Smart Carbs approach you will be getting these healthy saturated fats from grass-fed butter; grass-fed and sustainable red meat; coconut cream and milk; lard and tallow; coconut oil or MCT/keto oil; eggs; and cocoa butter.

Roughly half of our cell membrane structure is composed of saturated fat, and saturated animal fats, like grass-fed butter and fatty organ meats, contain large amounts of essential fat-soluble vitamins such as K, A, and D. So rather than getting them in pill form, it's great to know we can find them in real food.

Now, it's important to understand that not all fats are created equal, and we should be very careful to steer clear of unhealthy trans fats – the hydrogenated and partially hydrogenated oils found in processed products like cookies, crackers, margarine and fast food, as well as processed vegetable oils like cottonseed, sunflower, safflower, soybean and canola oils used by most takeaway shops and some restaurants. In brief, these fats are denatured, highly unstable, go rancid easily and can cause us great harm in the form of toxicity, inflammation and possible mineral deficiency. As with anything, we should try not to stress or worry about it, but simply make well-informed, mindful decisions when it comes to what we consume.

Fat is crucial for regulating carbohydrate metabolism, therefore assisting appropriate energy release.

FIGHTING FAT WITH FAT

When we find the right balance of carbohydrates, fats and proteins from real-food sources and limit our intake of processed, refined and sugary foods we become very effective fat-burning machines! Now, it can take 4–6 weeks to really see this kick in, but trust me, if you follow this way of eating your body will reset to its natural healthy state. However, please don't think that simply upping the fat in your diet while still consuming high amounts of sugar will yield the same results – you need to remove all excess and processed sugars from your diet, and keep your natural sugars low to get into the fat-burning zone. How do you best go about doing this? My advice is to learn to love the kitchen and embrace cooking! This will give you the most control over your health, wellness and happiness journey – enabling you to choose the best possible produce while avoiding any hidden nasties.

HITTING THE SWEET SPOT: UNDERSTANDING SUGAR

As my regular readers know, I certainly don't believe in stopping you from having a sweet treat! So the treat recipes in this book are full of delicious, naturally sweet ingredients that fit into our three carb zones. Understanding how to manage your sugar intake and sugar replacements is important, so let's take a look at the ones I recommend you use.

SWEETENERS TO LOVE

I use a small selection of natural sweeteners in my recipes, which are as follows:

- Green leaf stevia powder (sugar free)
- Freeze-dried berries/berry powder (low sugar)
- Coconut nectar/sugar
- Pure maple syrup
- Raw honey

Detailed below, these sweeteners are pretty much interchangeable in my recipes – if you'd rather use an alternative, just swap it and adjust the quantities to taste (being mindful of which zone you're eating from to achieve your goals, of course). As well as revealing which zone these sweeteners fall into and information on the net carbs per serve, the table below also lists each sweetener's glycemic index (GI) rating – a measurement of the impact that a food has on our blood-sugar levels.

	KETO	LOW-CARB	SUSTAIN		
	Green leaf stevia powder	Freeze-dried berry powder	Coconut sugar	Pure maple syrup	Raw honey
GI RATING	0 (low)	20–40 (low)	35 (low)	54 (medium)	45–65 (medium)
NET CARBS (per serve)	0 g (per ¼ teaspoon)	6 g (per tablespoon)	11 g (per tablespoon)	13.4 g (per tablespoon)	17.3 g (per tablespoon)

STEVIA

Commonly known as the 'sweet leaf', stevia is a herb whose extract is used as a sweetener and sugar substitute. Stevia belongs to a group of non-nutritive sweeteners, meaning it contains no calories, vitamins or any other nutrients.

Stevia is available in many forms, but my preference is for the powdered green leaf variety as a natural product rather than the refined/white variety. Some brands may leave a bitter aftertaste, so I suggest you try a few until you find the one you like. It's important to note that, depending on which one you choose, stevia can be between 200 and 300 times sweeter than sugar, so use it sparingly. And do check that your chosen product doesn't contain artificial sweeteners, dextrose, maltodextrin or even sugar – don't be fooled by the green packaging!

FREEZE-DRIED BERRIES

Berries are generally regarded as the most nutritious and lowest in starchy carbs of all the fruits. If you can find freeze-dried berries and berry powders without additives (good health-food stores should stock them), do give them a whirl – they are a great sweetener for smoothies, raw desserts and baked goods.

As well as sweetness, freeze-dried berries add lots of flavour to dishes and you will only need to use a very small amount, so you don't have to worry about excessive carbs. And when used to decorate desserts, whole or crushed freeze-dried berries can make them look spectacular. Freeze-dried raspberries are my favourite.

COCONUT SUGAR

Coconut sugar is derived from coconut palm blossom and has a slightly caramel taste and smell, making it a fantastic ingredient to use in baking. It is rich in minerals such as magnesium, potassium and zinc, while its sugar content is half fructose and half glucose. When looking for a healthy sweetener this is important because the lower the fructose content, the better (as excessive consumption of fructose can be addictive and lead to hormonal imbalance).

PURE MAPLE SYRUP

Now I am not talking about maple-flavoured syrups here but rather the pure syrup made from evaporated maple tree sap only. Unlike sugary maple-flavoured syrups, the pure stuff is high in zinc, which is important for optimal immune system function, as well as being rich in magnesium, calcium, B vitamins and antioxidants. Some might be surprised to see me recommending maple syrup as suitable for a low-carb approach, but as long as you are mindful of the quantity you consume, it is a good alternative to refined sugar.

RAW HONEY

Unfiltered raw honey is one of the most nutrient-dense of natural sweeteners. It differs from the processed types you find in supermarkets – where many of the essential nutrients honey contains are destroyed during pasteurisation and heating – so it is worth making the extra effort and picking up your jar from a speciality store, farmers' market or local farmer (if you're lucky enough to have one!).

The GI rating of honey can vary depending on the botanical source of the honey (with different blossoms yielding honey of varying sweetness). Because it contains a relatively high quantity of carbohydrate I recommend you include honey in your diet (in moderation) only when following a Sustain approach and steer clear of it when going into the Keto or Low-Carb zones.

BUT WHAT ABOUT...?

With the food industry catching up with our search for sugar-free or naturally sweetened alternatives, it is really important to be aware of what is actually going into some of these so-called 'healthier' options. Here are some I reckon you should be wary of.

RICE MALT SYRUP

Rice malt syrup is virtually fructose-free compared with honey, maple syrup and coconut sugar, making it very popular with the 'sugar-free' crew. It does, however, have a very high GI rating (98) – higher than regular sugar – which can lead to large blood-sugar spikes. It's for this reason that I steer clear of it.

AGAVE NECTAR

You'll see numerous health-food stores shouting from the rooftops about their sugar-free or refined sugar-free treats, which, on closer inspection, you'll find to be packed to the brim with agave nectar. Extracted from the blue agave cactus (which is also used to make tequila), agave nectar is made up of over 90% fructose, which has been proven to have damaging effects on our metabolism. Don't go near it.

XYLITOL

Xylitol is used in lots of keto and low-carb recipes these days as it provides a similar taste to regular sugar. I avoid it for a number of reasons, but mostly because it is highly poisonous and lethal to dogs in very small amounts, and I would never put my gorgeous Chia at risk by having it in the house!

ARTIFICIAL SWEETENERS

If you value your health, wellbeing and longevity, I strongly advise against using artificial sweeteners like aspartame, saccharin, acesulfame K or sucralose, due to the potential negative health effects that have been ascribed to these ingredients. They aren't real foods conducive to good health – steer clear.

MEALS, MINDSET AND MOVES

When you're striving for optimal health, wellbeing and happiness, I can't stress enough how important it is to find synergy between your meals, mindset and moves. Achieving a balance between these three elements will enable you to achieve fantastic results that are both sustainable and lasting.

THE MEALS

When I refer to 'the meals' I am essentially referring to all of the wonderful foods that are woven into the recipes here and in my other books. Celebrating nutrient-dense foods helps support us and enables us to thrive, while eliminating and avoiding foods that can cause harm or inflammation helps return our bodies to their natural state of wellbeing.

THE MINDSET

Eating well is all well and good, but if we're not thinking positively and backing ourselves then we're not really living to our true potential. I can speak firsthand of what it's like to experience stress and anxiety and the effects that this has on health. Similarly, when my mental health is under control, my health flourishes and everything, including the quality of my sleep, improves. Back yourself – and believe in yourself – and surround yourself with good people who believe in you, and you'll soon find yourself on the right track to making successful, sustainable long-term changes to your health and wellbeing.

THE MOVES

So you're starting to eat well and that voice inside your head has started to be more positive – GREAT! It's time to move, for so many reasons. Now, I am not talking about movement to burn calories – we all know you can't out-train a bad diet. Instead I am talking about making sure we get in that general, everyday movement that all of us, young and old alike, need to stay agile and functional. What shape should that take for you? Look to what you love – if that's a gym workout or a yoga class, great. Or it could simply be walking the dog. Whatever it is, make sure you find something you enjoy doing every day. Longevity is the key here.

WHY THE SMART CARBS APPROACH WORKS

1. THE RESULTS ARE QUICK AND EFFORTLESS

Finding the right balance of carbohydrates for you and your lifestyle works because the results are quick and tangible, helping you to stay on track and giving you the motivation needed to keep going. When a severely overweight person opts for the right zone, reduces the carbs and increases their healthy fat and well-sourced protein intake, and quickly loses 5 kg in the first week, they are more likely to adhere to the lifestyle for the long haul. Nothing feels better than results that are effortless!

2. YOU INCREASE THE NUTRIENT DENSITY OF YOUR FOOD

By upping your intake of all those great healthy fats and well-sourced proteins, you'll no longer have room for the usual 'fillers' in your diet, full of empty calories that don't even touch the sides. And making delicious swaps – like asking for the side salad rather than reaching for the dinner roll, or opting for roasted veggies instead of hot chips – won't just reduce the amount of carbs you eat but will also up your intake of nutrients, vitamins, minerals and phytochemicals, many of which have positive metabolic effects.

3. THOSE HEALTHY FATS HELP TO KEEP YOU ON TRACK

Healthy fats keep you feeling fuller for longer, which helps prevent snacking, eases cravings and reduces the chance of emotional eating. In addition, a diet higher in healthy fats is more likely to support hormonal balance and blood sugar regulation, so you won't feel like such a slave to what you eat.

4. YOU INCREASE YOUR PROTEIN INTAKE

Increasing your protein intake has many beneficial effects on health, including weight loss. Of all the macronutrients, protein increases satiation the most – meaning you'll no longer be fighting your own body's physiological desire for more food. Plus, increasing your protein intake encourages retention and growth of lean muscle mass, which results in greater resting energy expenditure, helping you burn more calories each day.

5. YOU CUT OUT REFINED SUGARS AND PROCESSED FOODS

Excessive consumption of sugary, processed foods takes its toll on our long-term health, causing energy dysfunction, mood irregularities and weight gain, and leading to complications including fatty liver disease – which can have terrible consequences for a person's metabolic health, insulin sensitivity, glucose tolerance and waistline. By removing refined sugars and processed foods from the diet we minimise the potential for these complications.

6. YOU DEPLETE YOUR BODY'S GLYCOGEN STORES

Glycogen is the main way the body stores glucose for later use. Unfortunately our storage capacity for this energy is limited, which is what causes many of our health-related problems – by not eating the right foods, these glycogen stores can become perpetually full to the brim, which means any excess carbohydrate we consume is converted into fat for storage in the liver, leading to weight gain. Reducing our carb intake drastically empties our body's glycogen stores and flicks the 'switch' for the body to stop using glycogen for energy and begin burning our fat reserves instead (see page 26 for more details).

7. IT'S DELICIOUS AND EASY TO FOLLOW

So many quick-fix diets seem to fail because people simply don't enjoy them enough to adhere to them long term. But with so much delicious food on offer when following my Smart Carbs approach, you won't be feeling like you're missing out. By eating food that you're excited about, you are far more likely to succeed in transforming your health for the better.

SMART CARBS AT A GLANCE

- **Decide which zone on the Smart Carb Curve is the best fit for you** Make this choice according to your lifestyle and health goals – whether that's a very low-carb Keto approach, a more flexible Low-Carb lifestyle, or the easy-to-follow Sustain route.

- **Stick to your chosen zone for a minimum of 6–8 weeks** This will allow you to build up an average baseline of consumption of the three major macronutrients (carbohydrates, fats and proteins). Only adjust this once you've really listened to your body and monitored your results.

- **Avoid inflammatory foods and toxins** All the recipes in this book are gluten free, dairy free and refined-sugar free – so if you enjoy these exclusively you'll be off to a good start! Be sure also to steer clear of toxic seed oils, foods high in added sugar, drugs and alcohol.

- **Stay hydrated** Getting enough water into your body promotes detoxification, can aid fat loss and supports your immune system and healthy hormonal function. So drink up!

- **Supplement if you need to, but keep it real** Real foods always win, so look at adding bone broths or fermented vegetables to your diet if you think you need a little something extra and go from there. Natural multivitamins, probiotics, omega-3 fish oils and natural protein powders may be beneficial for some people.

- **Start with the aim to Sustain first** If you're new to eating nutrient-dense real food and are getting into the kitchen for the first time after a lifestyle of fast and convenience foods, my advice is to focus on recipes in the Sustain Zone. This is an easy and manageable approach into this awesome new way of life and doesn't immediately limit or restrict your carbohydrate intake.

- **Celebrate herbs and spices** Apart from supplying your body with many health benefits, these can elevate your food to the next level, so be adventurous and try new flavour combinations – you'll find plenty of inspiration over the pages that follow!

- **Move frequently** While 80% of any health journey comes down to nutrition, incidental everyday exercise strengthens your cardiovascular and immune system, promotes efficient fat metabolism and gives you a strong base to handle more intense workouts. So take the stairs, walk the dog, and keep your body active as often as you can in everyday life. Think of this exercise as the added bonus to your healthy journey.

- **Look to reduce stress** This goes for both mental and physical stressors – find time to switch off the mind, and don't over-train your body. Not only will this improve your wellbeing, you will also find that reduced cortisol production as a result of being less stressed will enable you to shed excess body fat more easily. Win-win!

- **Remember, it's all about balance** Strive to achieve balance between the Meals, Mindset and Moves (see page 21) for optimal wellbeing inside and out. Remember that the best version of you cannot be found by obsessively focusing on one aspect or goal but instead requires a multi-pronged, complementary approach.

FREQUENTLY ASKED QUESTIONS

ARE PALEO AND KETO THE SAME THING?

No, but they can be very similar and follow a similar approach.

A paleo approach to eating – which is based on eliminating certain foods such as grains, beans, legumes, dairy and processed refined foods from the diet – is a lifestyle choice designed to reduce inflammation and support digestive health. The keto approach is more focused on increasing weight loss and improving cognitive function by placing the body into a metabolic state called ketosis, where your body begins to burn fatty acids rather than its usual energy source, glucose.

The approaches are similar in that they both encourage eating well-sourced grass-fed and organic animal proteins as well as plenty of non-starchy vegetables and leafy greens; focus on healthy fats such as nuts, seeds and animal fats; and avoid refined sugars, grains and legumes.

While both approaches can be used to achieve certain health outcomes, the keto diet is more rigorous and targeted, whereas a low-carb paleo approach is more of a long-term lifestyle choice that many find less restrictive and more sustainable. Here are the five main differences between the two:

1. **The paleo approach isn't necessarily low-carb, high-fat** When following a paleo approach there's no real limit to the amount of carbs you can eat when it comes to either fruit or starchy vegetables such as sweet potato and pumpkin. You can also use natural sweeteners that are higher in carbs such as raw honey, coconut nectar and pure maple syrup more liberally when following a purely paleo approach.

2. **The keto diet doesn't restrict dairy** Though this is typically the case, I have made sure all the keto recipes in this book are dairy free (apart from grass-fed butter, that is; see page 28 for an explanation). The reason for this is that an estimated 60–70% of us stop producing an adequate amount of lactase – the enzyme needed to digest lactose, the milk sugar found in dairy – in adulthood. This lack of lactase, and our inability to properly digest lactose, is what can make lactose-containing dairy products quite inflammatory to us. Dairy also contains the protein casein, which is one of the most difficult proteins for the body to digest and can trigger allergies and additional inflammation in some of us.

3. **The keto diet measures fat, protein, and carb percentage** In order for the keto diet to be effective and for the body to enter the desired state of ketosis, we must consume our macronutrients in a very specific ratio. The paleo approach is much more flexible about the ratio in which these macronutrients are consumed.

4. **The keto diet requires testing for ketosis** There are several testing methods for detecting ketone bodies in your blood that indicate whether your body has successfully begun to burn fatty acids for energy. The paleo approach doesn't have a specific metabolic goal – it's more of a lifestyle choice.

5. **The keto diet focuses on a specific energy source** It is concerned with the body burning fat rather than carbs, which is achieved by taking in the three macronutrients – carbohydrates, proteins and fats – in the correct ratio. The paleo approach does not focus on energy sources in this way.

The good news is you don't have to choose! This book is all paleo, while also giving you the option of following a strict Keto Zone approach (as well as Low-Carb and Sustain Zone approaches) if this is the best health choice for you and your lifestyle.

SHOULD EVERYONE GO VERY LOW-CARB OR KETO?

The short answer is no – you need to respect your bio-individuality and do what works for you and your lifestyle. Some people do perfectly fine on very low-carb or keto diets for years and years. If that happens to be you, great! But if that's not you, a Sustain Zone, real-food approach may be perfect for achieving your optimum state of wellbeing, healthy body weight and hormonal balance.

WHAT ARE LOW-CARB AND KETO DIETS SPECIFICALLY GOOD FOR?

Research has proved that low-carb and keto diets can be incredibly effective in helping to improve certain conditions, including (but not limited to):

- Overweight and obesity
- High blood sugar, metabolic syndrome, diabetes (both type 1 and type 2)
- Epilepsy
- Parkinson's disease
- Alzheimer's disease and other neurological conditions
- Polycystic ovary syndrome (PCOS)

Low-carb and keto diets have been proven to significantly improve certain major health conditions.

However, it is important to note that not everyone will (or indeed can) benefit from one particular dietary approach. We cannot ignore the important differences that determine what is optimal for each person with regard to their bio-individuality – these include variations in genes, activity levels, geography and much more. When it comes to diet, there is no one-size-fits-all approach.

CAN I EAT ANY FORM OF CARBOHYDRATE WHEN FOLLOWING A SUSTAIN ZONE APPROACH?

If you find yourself in the Sustain Zone, it is important to remember that real-food carbohydrates do not affect the body in the same way as processed and refined carbohydrates, therefore it's best to avoid the processed and refined options and stick with the good stuff suggested in my recipes.

We cannot treat all carbohydrates as if they're the same. Historically, most hunter-gatherer societies consumed about 25–45% of their calories from carbohydrates, while evidence in some specific ancestral populations puts this figure above 70%. Yet despite this liberal consumption of carbohydrates, these people were remarkably lean, fit and free of chronic, inflammatory diseases such as diabetes, cardiovascular disease, and neurological conditions. Their carbohydrates came from starchy tubers and plants, whole fruits and honey if they were lucky – all foods celebrated in my recipes. Never forget, when it comes to our three macronutrients, quality is much more important than quantity.

ARE CARBS BAD FOR ME?

The dietary advice we have received in the past two decades has contained many mixed messages about carbohydrates, leaving many of us who are simply looking to adopt a healthy approach to eating great food totally confused. Some of the proposed diets have demonised all carbs (including starchy veg and fruit) and have suggested banishing them from your life completely. Sure, removing processed and refined carbs is a great way of speeding up weight loss and dodging disease, but pulling all carbs from your diet can deprive you of foods that contain many of the important vitamins and minerals our bodies need to function at their best. The simple truth is, the right types of carbs can be great for you, so long as they form part of an approach that works for you and your health goals.

WILL I FEEL FLAT WHEN I GO LOW-CARB OR KETO?

The short answer is no. We may experience a detox phase or period of adjustment, but the nutrient-dense foods in my keto and low-carb recipes, which include healthy fats and well-sourced proteins, will actually provide us with a sustained source of energy by regulating blood-sugar levels. They will also assist in achieving appropriate hormonal balance and improved cognitive function, helping us power through the day. Plus, the healthier you are, the more likely you are to get some exercise, which increases the brain's uptake of the amino acid tryptophan, a precursor to your body's happy hormone, serotonin.

HOW DOES MY BODY GO INTO KETOSIS?

To answer this question, we must first understand the process of how our bodies transform fatty acids into energy:

1. Fatty acids (molecules found in healthy fats) are broken down into a compound called acetyl-CoA.
2. Acetyl-CoA combines with another compound called oxaloacetate.
3. The acetyl-CoA/oxaloacetate duo starts a sequence of reactions called the Krebs cycle
4. The Krebs cycle produces the molecule ATP, the body's energy currency.
5. Congratulations! You've just turned fat into energy.

Ketones are what we are after here, and we achieve them by the liver converting any excess acetyl-CoA (from fatty acids) into ketone bodies. These ketone bodies act as an alternative energy source for the brain and body, and this process places us in ketosis.

> When we are keto-adapted, we become more efficient at using fat and ketones for fuel, thereby saving our glycogen supplies for when we really need them.

HOW DO I KNOW I HAVE ENTERED KETOSIS?

A body in a state of ketosis generates elevated levels of ketones, which are detectable in the blood and urine. These can be picked up accurately using ketone urine testing strips, which are widely available from pharmacies. You may also notice a change in the way your breath smells, caused by the release of ketone bodies through respiration – don't mistake this for not brushing your teeth!

CAN GOING KETO OR LOW-CARB HELP IMPROVE MY BRAIN FUNCTION?

Research has shown that following a ketogenic diet can improve memory. A study of type-1 diabetics who experienced reduced cognitive function when their blood sugar was low found that by increasing their production of ketones through consuming the medium-chain triglycerides (MCTs) found in coconut oil (and sold as MCT oil in health-food stores) they could restore that cognitive function. Another test showed that increasing ketone levels for adults with bad memories improved their cognitive function.

HOW DO GLYCOGEN AND KETONES DIFFER AS ENERGY SOURCES?

Glycogen is a quick-release fuel which we store in the muscles and liver for intense physical exertion. We can only store about 2,400 calories of glycogen, however – enough for a couple of hours of intense activity at most – and once it's gone, we have to consume more carbs to restore our reserves. When we are keto-adapted, we become more efficient at using fat and ketones for fuel, thereby saving our glycogen supplies for when we really need them. Even very lean people carry tens of thousands of calories of excess body fat, so when we tap into this on a ketogenic diet our energy supplies become virtually limitless.

HOW LONG DOES IT TAKE TO GO KETO?

First off, be mindful that you're switching over to a new metabolic substrate. It can take some getting used to, so make sure you've eaten clean for some time beforehand so it isn't a complete shock to the body.

You'll want to make a minimum commitment to 6 weeks of nutritional ketosis. The first 3 weeks will be the most difficult as you switch over your fuel sources – and you may experience periods of cravings, lethargy, or irritability – but it should get easier from then on. People who take their exercise seriously may experience a temporary performance dip in the early weeks, but will come back strong after week 4 and beyond. Once you get to the 6-week mark, the metabolic machinery is in place, and it's hard to reverse the adaptation.

SHOULD I GO KETO LONG-TERM?

While going keto is certainly a great way to kick-start your body into burning excess body fat, it certainly isn't something I'd recommend indefinitely for most people. Not only is it unlikely to be manageable for your lifestyle, it is simply unnecessary for most healthy people – occasional or even regular dips into ketosis through fasting, very low-carb cycles or intense exercise are preferable and sufficient. Plus, cycling your ketosis means you can eat a wider variety of delicious foods seasonally. Above all else, listen to your body – if ketosis doesn't agree with your individual health or personal performance goals, then you might be better suited to a Low-Carb or Sustain Zone approach instead.

WILL I HAVE ENOUGH ENERGY TO TRAIN HARD WHILE GOING KETO?

Many people assume you need carbohydrates as fuel for training and recovery, but there is no evidence that carbohydrates increase gym performance any more than good-quality fat. In fact, being keto-adapted has several advantages for anyone interested in physical performance – it increases energy efficiency, while at any given intensity, a keto-adapted athlete will burn more fat and less glycogen than a sugar-burning athlete.

IS INTERMITTENT FASTING GOOD FOR ME?

Research has shown that intermittent fasting can be a very effective way of managing your body's insulin production, resulting in fat loss and increased energy levels. When you fast, you limit your body's need to produce insulin, which in turn can help normalise your blood-sugar levels and burn excess body fat.

If you're interested in fasting and want to dip your toe in the water, one easy place to start would be to try eating your dinner before 6 pm and then not consuming anything until after 10 am the next day. Approaches to fasting are highly individual, so whatever you do, be sure to listen to your body and always consult a health professional before undertaking this sort of diet or lifestyle change.

IS GLUTEN-FREE THE SAME AS LOW-CARB?

Absolutely not! In fact, most of the gluten-free products on the market (think gluten-free breads, pastas, cookies and treats) are actually higher in carbs than the standard products. Just because it says it is gluten-free doesn't mean it is good for you, so read your labels carefully, and remember the golden rule – if you're ever in doubt, just eat real food.

DOES LOW-FAT EQUAL LOW-CARB?

Absolutely not! When food producers and manufacturers remove the fat from a product they have to replace it with sugar to try to make that product taste good. Therefore, beware the old-fashioned 'low-fat' advertising tactics – you could easily be tricked into thinking you're eating something 'healthy' that actually contains more sugar per gram than a regular chocolate bar or sweet.

IF I'M MAKING HEALTHY FOOD CHOICES, CAN I EAT AS MUCH AS I WANT ON A LOW-CARB DIET?

I'm afraid the idea that you can eat an unlimited amount of food on a low-carb diet while still losing weight and staying healthy is a myth. No matter what diet you follow, overconsumption is never beneficial – it can prevent or stall weight loss and even cause weight gain. The good news is that, whichever carb approach you choose, you should find yourself easily satiated as a result of all the delicious healthy fats and good-quality proteins you are taking on board, so overconsumption shouldn't be a problem.

MAKING THE MOST OF THIS BOOK

This book takes my overall health principles to the next level, with plenty of delicious, nutritious and easy-to-prepare meal options no matter what the time of day or which carb approach you opt for. I've got you covered with loads of delicious options for all occasions. But how do you go about choosing what recipe works for you and your individual goals from a Smart Carbs point of view?

All the recipes in this book have been tagged with symbols that denote which carb zone (or zones) they sit in according to my Smart Carb Curve – whether that's Keto (K), Low-Carb (LC) or Sustain (S). Most recipes are really flexible and can be easily adjusted to suit your preferred zone – a Sustain recipe can often be made Low-Carb, for example, by swapping out below-ground starchy vegetables for above-ground lower-carb options, or by swapping a higher-GI sweetener like honey, maple syrup or coconut sugar for green leaf stevia – and many of the recipes include suggestions for doing exactly this. Whatever your health approach, I urge you not to feel restricted by a recipe or the zone that it has been tagged as – food is to be celebrated, and there is always a way to eat the amazing variety of delicious, nutrient-dense foods that this book celebrates while still achieving your goals. Some other extra little symbols that you will see are Nut-Free (NF), Vegan (V) and Raw (R), to make life a little easier for those who may have a nut allergy or are looking specifically for vegan or raw options. I've also included a special index at the back of the book (see page 266), which shows all of the Keto and Low-Carb recipes at a glance.

So, what about the specific ingredients I recommend you use? When it comes to cooking fats and oils, my three favourites are extra-virgin olive oil, coconut oil and grass-fed butter – interchangeable in most recipes, unless deep-frying where I opt for coconut oil. My use of butter despite promoting a largely dairy-free approach is due to the fact that full-fat, grass-fed butter contains next to no lactose, a sugar present in other dairy products that causes inflammation among certain people. If you do have a diagnosed dairy intolerance then you'd better stick with the other options on hand, but for the majority of us, grass-fed butter not only makes food taste delicious, it's good for us too!

In terms of animal proteins, choose good-quality, grass-fed beef; free-range, happy poultry and pork; and line-caught, sustainable fish and shellfish that come from ethical sources – as happy animals that eat natural diets lead to meats that contain the maximum nutritional content. Season with mineral-rich sea salt flakes or Himalayan pink salt and freshly ground black pepper for full flavour. If you come across an ingredient that you are not 100% familiar with (such as coconut aminos or cacao butter) don't be fazed by this – see it as an opportunity to either extend your repertoire and introduce yourself to something new and exciting or just leave it out. Check out your local health-food store or pop online.

As always, it's about shopping with care and respect, and having fun in the kitchen to produce epic food that is both healthy and delicious. Looking after yourself nutritionally should never feel like a chore or seem restrictive and lack flexibility. I believe it's about celebrating the variety of fantastic nutrient-dense foods we are so fortunate to have access to, voting with our dollar when it comes to supporting ethical and sustainable farming practices, and smiling each and every time you step into that kitchen, because that attitude will truly transform your health.

Happy cooking, legends!

Luke xx

BREAKFAST

The avocado mojito (K) (LC) (S) (NF) (V) (R)

SERVES 2

This rich and creamy avocado smoothie makes good use of those phenomenally delicious detoxifying ingredients, ginger and turmeric. It's also full of good fats and is high in antioxidants and anti-inflammatories.

1 avocado
250 ml (1 cup) coconut milk
1 handful of mint leaves,
   plus extra to garnish
3 tablespoons filtered water,
   plus extra if needed
½ teaspoon ground turmeric or
   5 mm piece of fresh turmeric,
   finely grated
1 teaspoon ground ginger or
   1 cm piece of ginger, finely
   grated
¼ teaspoon stevia
zest and juice of 1 lime
1 cup crushed ice

Place all the ingredients in a food processor or high-speed blender and whiz everything together until smooth (if it's a bit thick for your liking, loosen it up with a little extra water). Pour into glasses, garnish with extra mint leaves and serve.

THE LOWDOWN

One of the reasons I love adding mint to my recipes is because it is a great digestion aid, helping us better process and absorb the nutrients we take on board in all the food we eat. It can also soothe the stomach in cases of indigestion, inflammation or discomfort.

Healthy hormone shake (K) (LC) (S) (R)

SERVES 1

Want to balance your energy levels and boost your mood and brain function? Then look no further than this healthy hormone shake! It includes good-quality oil for energy and maca powder for its powerful hormone-balancing properties.

250 ml (1 cup) almond or
   coconut milk
1 tablespoon macadamia
   nut butter
1 tablespoon MCT oil (see page
   232), coconut oil or extra-virgin
   olive oil
2 teaspoons maca powder
¼ teaspoon ground cinnamon
25 g (1 tablespoon) hydrolysed
   powdered gelatine (optional)
¼ teaspoon stevia (optional)

Blitz all the ingredients in a food processor or high-speed blender until smooth. Pour into a glass over ice and enjoy!

THE LOWDOWN

Maca powder is available in health-food stores. It can help rebalance hormone levels and may increase libido and sexual function. If maca is a new ingredient for you, start with just 1 teaspoon to avoid potential digestive issues, and gradually add more as you get used to it.

Hydrolysed powdered gelatine provides a large range of amino acids and has excellent anti-inflammatory properties. It is available at health-food stores or online.

Dark choc and pink salt thickshake

SERVES 1

To my mind, nothing quite beats the bitterness of dark chocolate combined with mineral-rich pink salt – it's a flavour-match made in heaven. Sweetened with keto-friendly green-leaf stevia and filled with energy from good-quality fats and mood-boosting cacao, this nutrient-dense thickshake is the perfect way to start the day.

250 ml (1 cup) coconut milk
½ avocado
1 tablespoon cacao powder
¼ teaspoon ground cinnamon
¼ teaspoon stevia
½ vanilla pod, split and seeds
 scraped, or ½ teaspoon vanilla
 powder
2 tablespoons macadamia nut
 or peanut butter
generous pinch of pink
 Himalayan salt
4 ice cubes
cacao nibs, to serve (optional)

Blitz all the ingredients except the cacao nibs in a food processor or high-speed blender until smooth. Pour into a glass, garnish with a few cacao nibs (if using) and drink up!

TIP

Make it nut free in moments! Simply swap the macadamia nut or peanut butter for tahini for a delicious sesame flavour.

THE LOWDOWN

Both raw cacao and pink salt are rich sources of minerals, which I often refer to as the spark plugs of life! Similar to vitamins, they help our bodies grow, develop and stay healthy, performing many different functions from building strong bones and transmitting nerve impulses, to making hormones and even helping us maintain a normal heartbeat.

Pink dragon smoothie

SERVES 1

This vibrant smoothie is perfect for kids and the young at heart alike! It earns its name because when I was little I used to think kiwifruit were the same colour as dragons – so, by adding raspberries, we end up with … a pink dragon!

125 g (1 cup) raspberries,
 fresh or frozen
1 kiwifruit, peeled
250 ml (1 cup) coconut milk
25 g (1 scoop) hydrolysed
 powdered gelatine (optional)
1 tablespoon chia seeds
¼ teaspoon stevia
6 ice cubes

Put everything in a food processor or high-speed blender and whiz together until really well combined. Pour into a glass and drink straight away.

THE LOWDOWN

Did you know that one little kiwifruit contains more vitamin C than a lemon or orange? Yep! That's right. Plus, they aid digestion and are packed with vitamins and minerals that promote healthy, glowing skin.

Garlic and rosemary cauliflower bread

MAKES 1 LOAF

Breakfast has always been my favourite meal of the day – I often find myself thinking of it as I go to sleep, wondering what I will cook up the next morning. To my mind, there's not much better than having a loaf of this bread ready to go, either served up on its own or topped with yummy eggs or generous lashings of smashed avocado.

500 g (about 1 small head) cauliflower, outer leaves removed, broken into 4 cm florets
185 ml (¾ cup) coconut oil
2 garlic cloves, finely chopped
1 red onion, finely diced
½ teaspoon finely chopped rosemary, plus extra sprigs to garnish
6 eggs, at room temperature, plus 1 extra if needed
100 g (¾ cup) coconut flour
1 heaped teaspoon gluten-free baking powder
2 teaspoons sea salt
1 tablespoon sesame seeds

Preheat the oven to 200°C and line a 22 cm loaf tin with baking paper.

Add the cauliflower florets to a saucepan, cover with water and bring to the boil. Reduce the heat to a simmer and cook for 15 minutes, or until the florets are soft, then drain and set aside to dry.

Melt a tablespoon of the coconut oil in a frying pan over medium heat, add the garlic, onion and rosemary and cook, stirring regularly, for 3–4 minutes, or until the onion is caramelised and translucent.

Transfer the garlic, onion and rosemary mixture to a large bowl and whisk in the eggs, then add the coconut flour, baking powder and salt and mix well to combine, adding an extra egg if the mixture looks a little dry. Using a spoon, gently stir through the cauliflower, being careful not to break up the florets as you go (these give the bread its wonderful texture).

Pour the mixture into the prepared loaf tin, sprinkle over the sesame seeds and bake for 45 minutes, or until the top is golden brown and the loaf is set. To test, press down gently on the top of the loaf – if it holds its shape, it's ready. Remove from the oven and leave to cool slightly in the tin before turning out, slicing and serving.

Store in an airtight container for up to 5 days in the fridge or up to 3 months in the freezer. If not eating straight away, toast under the grill for best results.

TIP

Coconut flour can sometimes be a tricky ingredient to work with as it is very absorbent and different brands can vary in density. Whichever you choose, I suggest you use your intuition when cooking with it and add extra eggs or coconut oil to help moisten your ingredients if need be.

Low-carb breakfast loaf (LC) (S)

MAKES 1 LOAF

Bread is such a staple in our modern diets that it's often the thing people struggle to give up most when following a lower-carb approach. Cue this recipe, which is the perfect way for you to get your bread 'fix' without all those carbs! While almond meal can be a little dry on its own, adding psyllium husk helps to give your loaf a beautiful, moist consistency that leaves it tasting just like the real thing, while also helping to add loads of lovely fibre to your meal.

200 g (2 cups) almond meal
3 tablespoons ground psyllium
  husk
1 teaspoon sea salt
1 tablespoon gluten-free baking
  powder
4 large eggs, beaten
3 tablespoons coconut oil, melted
125 ml (½ cup) warm filtered
  water

Preheat the oven to 180°C and line a 22 cm loaf tin with baking paper.

In a bowl, mix together the almond meal, psyllium, salt and baking powder until well combined. Add the eggs, melted coconut oil and warm water and mix well to form a thick batter.

Pour the batter into the prepared loaf tin and bake for 45 minutes, or until golden brown and cooked through. To test, press down gently on the top of the loaf – if it holds its shape, it's ready.

Remove the loaf from the oven and leave to cool completely in the tin. Enjoy straight away slathered with butter or nut butter or topped with scrambled eggs or, if eating later, toast under the grill for best results. To store, wrap in plastic wrap or keep in an airtight container in the fridge for up to 5 days.

THE LOWDOWN

If anyone ever comes to me looking for a digestive aid, psyllium husk is always my first recommendation. Its heart healthy, blood-sugar-balancing properties will keep your digestive system functioning wonderfully.

Tiramisu no grain-ola

MAKES 12 SERVES

This breakfast is my idea of heaven. I love the wonderful crunch you get from homemade granola, and here I've combined it with my all-time favourite ingredient, chocolate, along with a hit of delicious coffee. It's everything you know and love about tiramisu, served up in your morning bowl.

160 g (1 cup) almonds, roughly chopped
100 g (1 cup) pecans, roughly chopped
160 g (1 cup) macadamia nuts, roughly chopped
140 g (1 cup) pumpkin seeds
60 g (1 cup) coconut flakes
3 tablespoons cacao powder
2 tablespoons cacao nibs, plus extra to serve
1 teaspoon ground cinnamon
1 vanilla pod, split and seeds scraped, or 1 teaspoon vanilla powder
1 teaspoon sea salt
125 ml (½ cup) melted coconut oil or butter
125 ml (½ cup) espresso or filter coffee
3 tablespoons pure maple syrup
Whipped Vanilla Coconut Cream (see page 262), to serve

Preheat the oven to 180°C and line two baking trays with baking paper.

Add the dry ingredients to a large bowl and mix well to combine. In a separate bowl, whisk together the wet ingredients. Add the wet ingredients to the dry ingredients and mix everything together well, making sure the nuts and seeds are really well coated with the liquid.

Spread the mixture evenly over the prepared baking trays and bake for 10–15 minutes, or until the nuts are golden brown and the mixture is nice and dry.

Remove the trays from the oven and leave to cool, then transfer to an airtight container and store in the fridge for up to 1 week. To serve, top with whipped vanilla coconut cream and a scattering of cacao nibs.

THE LOWDOWN

Coffee isn't just something to wake you up in the morning – when consumed in moderation it has been shown to reduce the risk of type-2 diabetes and heart disease, and is high in antioxidant-rich ingredients. What's not to love?

Green brekky coleslaw

SERVES 2

This recipe is a wonderful way of incorporating some delicious raw vegetables into your diet. Packed with a wide range of colourful nutrients, the coleslaw has a fantastic crunchy texture that is balanced out perfectly by the creamy avocado dressing and the delicious boiled eggs that finish everything off. It's a great start to any day.

4 eggs
1 carrot, cut into matchsticks
¼ red cabbage, finely shredded
¼ white cabbage, finely shredded
1 green apple, cut into matchsticks
sea salt and freshly ground
   black pepper
dried chilli flakes, to serve
   (optional)

Dressing
1 avocado, mashed
3 tablespoons extra-virgin olive oil
3 tablespoons finely chopped
   flat-leaf parsley leaves
zest and juice of 1 lemon
1 tablespoon apple cider vinegar

Place the eggs in a small saucepan and cover with cold water. Cover with a lid and bring to the boil, then reduce the heat to medium and simmer gently for 3 minutes for soft-boiled eggs or 7 minutes for hard-boiled. Remove the eggs from the pan with a slotted spoon and leave to cool, then peel, halve lengthways and set aside.

Add the carrot, cabbage and apple to a large bowl and mix together to combine.

To make the dressing, combine all the ingredients in a small bowl and mix together well.

Using your hands, massage the avocado dressing into the coleslaw to evenly coat the individual veg pieces. Season with salt and pepper to taste. Divide between plates and serve topped with the boiled eggs and a sprinkling of chilli flakes, if you like.

THE LOWDOWN

Raw veggies are nutritional powerhouses that assist us with everything from healthy weight maintenance and heart health to helping to protect us from certain illnesses including cancer. It's really important to include raw vegetables in our diet as they contain important enzymes that assist our digestion. When we overcook vegetables, we essentially deactivate the enzymes, which means our pancreas and other digestive organs need to work harder to produce our own. Also, we know that the vitamins and antioxidants in fresh raw veggies are uncompromised and the fibre hasn't been broken down by cooking.

Cauliflower porridge (LC) (S)

SERVES 2

There is nothing better than starting the day with a bowl of nourishing porridge – and with this grain- and dairy-free alternative even those who avoid the traditional oat-based version can indulge. Those cooler mornings have this recipe written all over them!

400 g (2 cups) Cauliflower Rice
  (see page 262)
500 ml (2 cups) coconut cream
2 tablespoons desiccated coconut
½ ripe banana, mashed
1 teaspoon honey or pure maple
  syrup, plus extra to serve
1 vanilla pod, split and seeds
  scraped, or 1 teaspoon vanilla
  powder
½ teaspoon ground cinnamon

To serve
125 g (1 cup) raspberries (fresh
  or frozen and defrosted)
60 g (½ cup) roughly chopped
  toasted walnuts or pecans

Add all the ingredients to a saucepan set over medium–low heat and stir to combine. Cook for 6–8 minutes, stirring, until the cauliflower begins to soften and the mixture loosens up a little.

Bring to a simmer, then reduce the heat to low, cover with a lid and cook for another 15 minutes, stirring occasionally to prevent the mixture from sticking to the bottom of your saucepan, until thick and creamy. Remove from the heat, divide between bowls and serve topped with raspberries and nuts, and an extra drizzle of honey or maple syrup.

THE LOWDOWN

Cauliflower has got to be one of my all-time favourite vegetables. It's low carb and packed with vitamins and minerals but, most importantly, it's super versatile and can be transformed into pretty much anything – from this porridge to thin, crispy pizza bases (see page 169)!

Coconut choc–crunch cereal

MAKES 8 SERVES

When I was growing up, breakfast was all about which crunchy, sweet cereal we had in the house – I remember racing to the pantry, crossing my fingers that it would be one of those chocolate varieties, in which case all my dreams would have come true! This recipe is perfect for kids as well as adults who just want to feel young again – it's everything you could ask for in a breakfast cereal, without any of the processed and refined ingredients, of course.

60 g (1 cup) shredded coconut
60 g (½ cup) sunflower seeds
3 tablespoons chia seeds
1 tablespoon ground cinnamon
1 tablespoon cacao powder
¼ teaspoon sea salt
1 large egg
3 tablespoons honey or
  pure maple syrup
1 tablespoon coconut oil, melted

To serve
coconut or almond milk
Whipped Vanilla Coconut Cream
  (see page 262)
blueberries

Start by preheating the oven to 180°C and lining a baking sheet with baking paper.

Add the coconut, sunflower seeds, chia seeds, cinnamon, cacao and salt to a blender or food processor and whiz together to a fine flour consistency.

In a bowl, whisk the egg, honey or maple syrup and coconut oil together until well combined. Pour the wet ingredients into the prepared dry ingredients and mix well to form a lovely batter.

Spoon the batter into the centre of the prepared baking sheet. Cover with another piece of baking paper and use a rolling pin to roll it out to a thickness of about 5 mm. Remove the top layer of baking paper and score the dough with a sharp knife into 1 cm squares (this will help it break apart more easily after cooking).

Bake for about 20 minutes, or until dark and crispy. Remove from the oven and leave to cool completely on the sheet, then break apart into squares.

Serve with your choice of milk, whipped vanilla coconut cream and fresh blueberries. The cereal will keep stored in an airtight container in the fridge for up to 7 days.

THE LOWDOWN

One of the (many) things I love about chia seeds is that almost all of the carbs they contain come in the form of fibre, which is essential for our bodies to function well. They also aren't digested by the body like regular carbs so they don't raise blood sugar levels. In addition, chia seeds are also made up of a whopping 65 per cent omega-3 fatty acids, which our body looks to burn as a back-up energy source when following a low-carb diet. That makes them a win-win, in my book!

Layered pudding parfait ⓢ

SERVES 2

I know what you're thinking, and I can't blame you for wondering if you stumbled across the wrong chapter, but I can assure you this is a delicious breakfast and not a dessert. The thing I love about food is that any meal of the day can be bright, fun and healthily sweet, which is why this layered pudding parfait has your name written all over it.

125 ml (½ cup) almond or
   coconut milk
2 teaspoons honey or pure
   maple syrup
2 tablespoons cacao powder
2 tablespoons chia seeds
½ teaspoon vanilla extract
½ teaspoon ground cinnamon
pinch of salt
½ banana, sliced into discs
2 tablespoons peanut butter
   (or other nut butter)
70 g (½ cup) sliced strawberries,
   blueberries and/or raspberries
   (fresh or frozen and thawed)
2 tablespoons sliced toasted
   almonds

In a food processor, combine the almond or coconut milk, honey or maple syrup, cacao powder, chia seeds, vanilla, cinnamon and salt and blitz until smooth. Transfer to a bowl, cover with plastic wrap and refrigerate overnight.

To assemble your parfait, get two tall glasses or jars and cover the bottoms with strawberry or banana slices, then dollop over the nut butter. Divide the pudding mixture equally between the glasses and top with the mixed berries and toasted almonds to finish. Serve straight away or cover and store in the fridge for up to 3 days.

Nuts about bircher

SERVES 2

My number one breakfast – the one I would always order without fail at cafes – used to be bircher muesli. Nowadays I steer clear so as to avoid the grains and also because I'm not keen on consuming the level of carbohydrates the typical bircher contains, especially when so many are soaked in both yoghurt and apple juice. Thankfully, I have this delicious low-carb, grain- and dairy-free alternative to fall back on!

250 ml (1 cup) almond or
    coconut milk
2 tablespoons white chia seeds
2 tablespoons roughly chopped
    pecans or walnuts
2 tablespoons roughly chopped
    almonds
2 tablespoons roughly chopped
    sunflower seeds
2 tablespoons shredded coconut
2 green apples, cored and grated
zest and juice of 1 lemon
½ teaspoon ground cinnamon

To serve
2 tablespoons Whipped Vanilla
    Coconut Cream (see page 262)
    or coconut yoghurt
3 tablespoons blueberries

Mix all the ingredients together in a bowl to combine, then cover with plastic wrap and place in the fridge overnight.

Serve the next morning topped with whipped vanilla coconut cream and blueberries.

Note: to make this recipe low carb, simply swap the apple for kiwifruit or delicious, vibrant berries.

TIPS

To make a nut-free version simply swap out the nuts for pumpkin seeds and add some extra sunflower seeds and shredded coconut.

This keeps really well in an airtight container in the fridge for 3–4 days – try making it in bulk so that you have some bircher on hand for the rest of the week.

Keto Mexican scramble

SERVES 1

Super quick and simple, these delicious Mexican scrambled eggs mean there really is no excuse for not having a lovely cooked breakfast, even on busy mornings!

1 tablespoon coconut oil or butter
½ red onion, finely diced
1 garlic clove, finely chopped
1 bird's eye chilli, finely chopped
1 streaky bacon rasher, roughly chopped
1 tablespoon smashed avocado
1 tablespoon finely chopped coriander leaves, plus extra to serve
3 eggs, beaten
½ tomato, roughly chopped
sea salt and freshly ground black pepper
juice of ½ lime (optional)

Melt the coconut oil or butter in a frying pan over medium–high heat. Add the onion, garlic, chilli and bacon and cook, stirring often, for 5 minutes, or until the onion has softened and the bacon is cooked.

Meanwhile, combine the smashed avocado and coriander in a small bowl and set aside.

Pour the egg into the pan, add the tomato and cook, gently folding with a spatula as you go, until you have a soft scramble.

Slide the scrambled eggs into a bowl, season with salt and pepper and top with the smashed avo and extra coriander. Squeeze over a little lime juice, if you like, and enjoy.

THE LOWDOWN

Those of you familiar with my recipes will by now have cottoned on to the fact that I adore chilli! And for good reason – not only does it give a recipe a delicious kick, it also helps to aid digestion, and fresh chilli is packed full of vitamin C and can help relieve migraines and muscle, joint and nerve pains. What's not to love?

BRUNCH

Gorgeous green omelette with lemon–macadamia ricotta (K) (LC) (S)

SERVES 1

I am always looking for ways to help people get more greens into their diet and this green omelette is one of the easiest and tastiest ways I know of making that happen! It looks incredibly vibrant on the plate and every mouthful bursts with flavour and nutrients.

3 large eggs, beaten
50 g baby spinach leaves
1 tablespoon roughly chopped
  flat-leaf parsley leaves
3 tablespoons coconut cream
1 tablespoon coconut oil
2 handfuls of kale, stalks removed
  and leaves roughly chopped
1 tablespoon extra-virgin olive oil,
  coconut oil or butter
1 teaspoon finely chopped chives
sea salt and freshly ground
  black pepper

Lemon–macadamia ricotta
320 g (2 cups) macadamia nuts
1 teaspoon sea salt
zest and juice of 1 lemon
125 ml (½ cup) filtered water,
  plus extra if needed

To make the lemon–macadamia ricotta, put all the ingredients in a food processor and puree to a paste, scraping down the side of the bowl with a spatula halfway through to ensure everything gets mixed together well. Add a little extra water if you need to loosen it up a little – you're looking for a wet, chunky consistency like that of traditional ricotta. Transfer to a bowl and set aside. Wipe the processor bowl clean.

Preheat the oven to 90°C.

Add the egg, spinach, parsley, coconut cream, coconut oil and half the kale to the food processor bowl and blitz until well combined and a vibrant green colour.

Heat the oil or butter in a frying pan over medium heat. Pour in the egg mixture and, using a rubber spatula, gently stir, while tilting the pan and moving it back and forth over the heat at the same time. (This keeps the egg mix from sticking or browning.) After 4–5 minutes, or once the egg starts to set on top, slide the omelette onto a plate and transfer to the oven to keep warm.

Increase the stove heat to high, add the remaining kale to the same pan and saute for 3–4 minutes, or until slightly softened and charred around the edges.

To serve, top the omelette with 2 tablespoons of the lemon–macadamia ricotta, add the kale and sprinkle over the chives. Season with salt and pepper to taste and enjoy.

TIPS

Leftover macadamia ricotta can be stored in an airtight container in the fridge for up to 7 days. Try it spread on my breakfast breads, tossed through salads or on pizzas (see page 169).

If you don't have a food processor, you can either put everything in a bowl and use a hand-held blender to whiz together or else chop your greens super fine and use a whisk to incorporate them into the egg mixture.

Luscious low-carb crepes with lemon butter (LC) (S) (NF)

MAKES 4 LARGE CREPES

It's not often that you get to enjoy the delicious, sweet taste of crepes without taking on board the processed and sugary ingredients that come with the traditional kind. Thankfully this recipe has you sorted – offering up a low-carb option that will make your tummy smile!

1 egg yolk
4 egg whites
1 tablespoon coconut flour
2 teaspoons psyllium husk
45 ml coconut milk or
  coconut cream
½ teaspoon cream of tartar
¼ teaspoon gluten-free baking
  powder
1 tablespoon honey or
  pure maple syrup
pinch of salt
4–5 tablespoons extra-virgin
  olive oil, coconut oil or butter

Lemon butter
40 g butter, softened
zest and juice of 1 lemon

To make the lemon butter, add the softened butter and lemon zest and juice to a bowl and mix well to combine. Cover with plastic wrap and transfer to the fridge to chill and firm up.

Preheat the oven to 90°C.

Mix all the ingredients except the oil or butter in a large bowl to form a light, fluffy batter. Cover with plastic wrap and set aside for 5–10 minutes to thicken slightly, then whisk again to remove any lumps.

Heat 1–2 tablespoons of oil or butter in a frying pan over medium heat. Ladle one quarter of the batter into the pan and spread it out by tilting the pan to ensure it coats the base in a thin, even layer. (If you find at this stage that your batter is too thick to spread thinly, stir a tablespoon of water into the remaining mixture to loosen it up.) Cook for 1–2 minutes, or until firm, then use a spatula to flip over carefully. Cook for a further 1 minute, or until golden brown, then remove from the pan and keep warm in the oven. Repeat with the remaining batter, adding an extra tablespoon or so of oil or butter to the pan between crepes to make sure they don't stick to the bottom.

Serve the crepes spread with generous dollops of the lemon butter.

Note: to make these keto, simply swap the honey or maple syrup for ¼ teaspoon of green leaf stevia.

TIP

Once cool, the crepes can be stored in an airtight container in the fridge for up to 5 days.

Perfect pizza (LC) (S) (NF)

SERVES 2

I believe pizza is something you should enjoy any time of day and I think this recipe makes the perfect brunch! Everything you love about breakfast, combined with that pizza you want for lunch? You've got yourself a brunch pizza. You're welcome.

2 zucchini, grated and squeezed of excess liquid
3 tablespoons coconut flour
1 teaspoon dried Italian herbs
pinch of salt
4 eggs
2 tablespoons tomato paste
1 roma tomato, sliced
2 streaky bacon rashers, chopped
2 tablespoons basil leaves
1 handful of rocket leaves
2 tablespoons Lemon–Macadamia Ricotta (see page 58) (optional)
1 tablespoon extra-virgin olive oil

Preheat the oven to 180°C and line a pizza tray with baking paper.

Add the zucchini, coconut flour, Italian herbs, salt and two of the eggs to a bowl and mix together well to form a batter. Mould into the prepared pizza tray and bake for 6–8 minutes, or until par-baked.

Remove the base from the oven and spread the tomato paste evenly over the surface. Lay over the tomato slices and bacon, then carefully crack over the remaining eggs towards the centre to ensure they don't drip over the side. Transfer to the oven and bake for a further 5 minutes, or until the eggs are cooked.

Remove the pizza from the oven and top with the basil, rocket and lemon–macadamia ricotta (if using). Drizzle over the olive oil and serve.

THE LOWDOWN

Zucchini are great – not only are they widely available, inexpensive and seriously versatile in the kitchen, they are also really high in energy-rich B vitamins, vitamin A, vitamin C, calcium and magnesium, as well as being super low-carb and full of anti-inflammatory compounds.

Broccoli toasties

MAKES 6 OPEN SANDWICHES

In my book Healthy Made Easy I introduced you to my famous cauliflower toast. Now here, in the spirit of getting you guys eating more greens, are my awesome broccoli toasties! I love this recipe as it is truly fool-proof and can be used with a variety of different toppings.

4 eggs, beaten
½ head of broccoli, grated
55 g (½ cup) almond meal
55 g (½ cup) linseed meal
pinch of sea salt

Toppings
smoked salmon
avocado slices
Lemon–Macadamia Ricotta
  (see page 58)
herbs or salad leaves
sliced tomato
squeeze of lemon juice

Preheat the oven to 180°C and line a baking tray with baking paper.

In a bowl, mix all the ingredients together to form a thick dough. Transfer to the prepared baking tray and, using your fingers, press it out into a rectangle about 1 cm thick.

Bake in the oven for 30 minutes, or until golden brown and cooked through. Remove from the oven and leave to cool completely, then slice into six pieces.

To serve, load up the broccoli toasties with the toppings in any order you like or use your own favourite toast toppings. Enjoy!

TIPS

To make this recipe nut free, simply swap the almond meal for a seed-based meal.

This broccoli bread will keep in an airtight container in the fridge for up to 7 days or in the freezer for up to 3 months, so it's a good recipe to make in bulk.

THE LOWDOWN

It might surprise you to hear that broccoli contains omega-3 fatty acids – the type of fatty acids that make up a great source of fuel when following a low-carb diet. Our body thrives off these fatty acids, which can improve everything from cognitive function to energy levels.

Nasi goreng (LC)(S)(NF)

SERVES 2

Nasi goreng is a very well-known dish that hails from Indonesia, where it is commonly eaten for breakfast. It translates literally as 'fried rice', though my version switches out the standard white rice for cauliflower rice and uses other paleo alternatives, where necessary, to pack in the dish's famous flavours. My top tip here is to have all of your ingredients prepped and ready to go before you start cooking.

2 tablespoons extra-virgin olive oil, coconut oil or butter

10 raw prawns, shelled, deveined and diced

2 chicken thigh fillets, cut into 5 cm chunks

½ brown onion, finely diced

2 garlic cloves, finely chopped

1 long red chilli (or 2 bird's eye chillies if you like it hot)

1 carrot, finely diced

600 g (3 cups) Cauliflower Rice (see page 262)

1 tablespoon pure maple syrup

3 tablespoons coconut aminos or tamari

1 teaspoon sugar-free fish sauce

sea salt

To serve
2 fried eggs
1 handful of coriander leaves
freshly ground black pepper

Heat 1 tablespoon of oil or butter in a deep frying pan or wok over high heat. Add the prawns and stir-fry, tossing regularly, for 2 minutes, or until almost cooked through. Remove from the pan and set aside on a large plate.

Add the chicken to the pan and stir-fry for 4–5 minutes, or until lightly golden and cooked through, then remove from the pan and transfer to the plate with the prawns.

Add the remaining oil or butter to the pan and reduce the heat to medium. Stir-fry the onion, garlic and chilli for 2–3 minutes, or until softened and caramelised, then add the carrot, cauliflower rice, maple syrup, coconut aminos or tamari and fish sauce. Season with salt and stir to combine, then return the prawns and chicken to the pan and cook, stirring, for another 2–3 minutes.

Divide the 'fried rice' between two plates and top each with a fried egg, a scattering of coriander leaves and freshly ground black pepper. Serve immediately.

TIP

If you're new to my recipes you might be wondering what I mean when I refer to coconut aminos. Well, it's a delicious and healthy sauce made from coconut sap – salty and slightly sweet in flavour, it resembles a light soy sauce but it is soy- and gluten-free; making it the perfect replacement for those following a paleo or reduced-carb approach. It is available at most good health-food stores.

Easy stuffed mushrooms

MAKES 4

Stuffed mushrooms are one of the easiest yet most delicious meals you can put together. A great start to the day or a fuss-free lunch, this recipe is a celebration of simple flavours that go really well together on the plate.

4 large portobello mushrooms, stems removed and reserved
2 garlic cloves, very finely chopped
3 tablespoons crushed pecans
zest and juice of 1 lemon, plus extra zest to garnish
sea salt
100 ml extra-virgin olive oil
1 bunch of flat-leaf parsley leaves, roughly chopped
freshly ground black pepper
2 tablespoons pecans, toasted and roughly chopped

Preheat the oven to 200°C and line a baking tray with baking paper.

Add the mushroom stems, garlic, crushed pecans, lemon zest and juice, ½ teaspoon of salt and 3 tablespoons of the olive oil to a food processor, along with the parsley, reserving a tablespoon or so for garnish, and pulse together briefly to form a rough, wet paste.

Arrange the mushrooms, gill-side up, on the prepared baking tray and spoon over the prepared mixture. Drizzle over the remaining oil and bake for 20–25 minutes, or until the mushrooms are soft and cooked through and the herb crust is golden brown.

Divide among plates, season with salt and pepper and serve topped with the toasted pecans, extra lemon zest and reserved chopped parsley.

TIP

If you like the look of this for lunch but think you might need a little extra protein, try topping it with a runny poached egg.

THE LOWDOWN

Mushrooms are a good source of protein, vitamin C and iron. But did you know that the cell walls of mushrooms are made of chitin, which is largely indigestible by humans? Cooking mushrooms helps to break the cells open, making their nutritional contents more easily accessible to us.

Homemade crumpets

MAKES 4

I have such fond memories of coming home from primary school and walking into the house only to smell the aroma of freshly toasted crumpets for afternoon tea. These taste just like the ones you know and love but are completely paleo friendly – I love them with butter and honey, but feel free to add your favourite toppings of choice.

250 ml (1 cup) tepid filtered water
1 x 7 g sachet or 2 teaspoons dried yeast
125 g (1 cup) arrowroot or tapioca flour
80 g (¾ cup) almond meal
3 tablespoons fine granulated coconut sugar
1 tablespoon gluten-free baking powder
½ teaspoon sea salt
2 large eggs, beaten
125 ml (½ cup) canned coconut milk
3–4 tablespoons coconut oil or butter

Toppings
butter
honey or pure maple syrup

Pour the water into a glass measuring jug, add the dried yeast and stir to combine. Set aside for 10 minutes to allow the yeast to activate.

Whisk together the arrowroot or tapioca flour, almond meal, coconut sugar, baking powder and sea salt in a bowl. Add the egg and coconut milk and whisk together to form a smooth batter, then pour in the prepared yeast and water mixture and whisk again to combine.

Preheat the oven to 170°C. Lightly grease four egg rings.

Warm a tea towel by carefully placing it under very hot running water and then wringing it out to dry, or by soaking and draining it under cool water, then placing it in the microwave on high for 2 minutes. Cover the bowl with the warm tea towel and leave it to sit for 15 minutes until bubbly, then remove the tea towel and give the batter a final whisk.

Melt the oil or butter in a frying pan over medium heat. Place the egg rings in the pan and ladle the mixture evenly into them. Cook for 5 minutes (you should see the trademark airy holes begin to form), then transfer to the oven and cook for a further 15 minutes.

Remove the egg rings, then flip the crumpets and transfer to serving plates. Top with generous lashings of butter and drizzle with honey or maple syrup, if you like.

TIP

Dried yeast can be found in all supermarkets and health-food stores and comes either in handy packets containing 7 g sachets (making it perfect for recipes like this) or larger tubs which will need measuring out. If you haven't cooked with it before and are worried about cooking outside of your comfort zone, I can assure you it is really easy – give it a go here and you'll soon be reaping the taste rewards!

Pumpkin fritters with zucchini hummus (LC)(S)

SERVES 4

This is one of my favourite things to cook – the combo of super crispy fritters and zesty, fresh hummus is pretty much perfect! Try it once and I promise you'll soon be making it every week, like me.

600 g butternut pumpkin, peeled and cut into small pieces
2 large eggs, beaten
1 garlic clove, very finely chopped
3 tablespoons finely chopped flat-leaf parsley leaves
3 tablespoons almond meal
3 tablespoons arrowroot or tapioca flour
sea salt and freshly ground black pepper
2 tablespoons extra-virgin olive oil or coconut oil
sesame seeds, to serve
micro herbs, to serve (optional)

Zucchini hummus
150 g zucchini (1 medium-sized), cut lengthways into thick ribbons
3 tablespoons flat-leaf parsley or mint leaves
zest and juice of 1 lemon
1 garlic clove
1 tablespoon extra-virgin olive oil, plus extra to drizzle
1 tablespoon tahini
¼ teaspoon freshly ground black pepper
¼ teaspoon sea salt

Preheat the oven to 200°C and line a baking tray with baking paper.

To make the zucchini hummus, arrange the zucchini ribbons on the prepared baking tray in a single layer and roast for 10–15 minutes, or until lovely and softened. Transfer the zucchini pieces to a food processor with the remaining ingredients and blitz to a smooth puree. Set aside.

For the fritters, set a steamer over a saucepan filled with a little water and bring to the boil. Add the pumpkin, cover with a lid and steam for 3–5 minutes, or until tender. Transfer to a bowl and mash with a fork, then add the egg, garlic, parsley, almond meal and arrowroot or tapioca flour. Mix well to form a smooth batter. Season to taste.

Heat the oil in a frying pan over medium heat. Working in batches, carefully lower heaped tablespoons of the batter into the pan and gently flatten with a spatula. Fry for 8–10 minutes, turning halfway through cooking, until golden brown and cooked through. Remove from the pan and drain on paper towel.

Divide the fritters among plates, top with dollops of zucchini hummus and sprinkle sesame seeds and micro herbs (if using) over the top. Enjoy.

THE LOWDOWN

Pumpkin contains a wide range of nutrients including calcium, magnesium, potassium, vitamin A, copper and zinc. Many people are surprised to discover that it is also a great low-carb vegetable option – I love to use it as an alternative to sweet potato in recipes as it provides a similar sweet taste without the same level of starchy carbs.

Bangin' bruschetta

SERVES 4

Bruschetta is the name given to Italian toasted bread slices that are typically drenched in olive oil and topped with garlic and tomatoes. My version swaps out the bread for sweet potato and mixes up the toppings to deliver one of the best brunches you'll ever have!

1 large sweet potato
2 tablespoons extra-virgin olive oil, plus extra to drizzle
sea salt and freshly ground black pepper
2 teaspoons apple cider vinegar
4 eggs
2 avocados, roughly chopped
¼ red onion, roughly chopped
1 continental cucumber, roughly chopped
2 tablespoons finely chopped chives (optional)
200 g smoked salmon
1 teaspoon dried chilli flakes

Preheat the oven to 180°C and line a baking tray with baking paper.

Using a sharp knife or a mandoline, cut your sweet potato lengthways into four even slices approximately 1 cm thick. (Save the offcuts for roasting, adding to a curry or making chips!)

Coat both sides of the sweet potato slices generously with the olive oil and place on the prepared baking tray, then season with salt and bake for 30 minutes, or until golden brown and cooked through.

Meanwhile, add the apple cider vinegar to a large saucepan filled with water and bring to the boil. Reduce to a simmer, crack in the eggs and poach for 4–5 minutes, or until the whites are completely cooked. Carefully remove the eggs from the water with a slotted spoon and transfer to paper towel to remove any excess water.

Combine the avocado, red onion, cucumber and chives (if using) in a bowl.

Divide your sweet potato slices among plates and top with the smoked salmon, avocado mixture and poached eggs. Scatter over the chilli flakes, season with salt and pepper and serve.

THE LOWDOWN

Sweet potatoes contain high levels of beta-carotene, which gives them their orange colour. Our bodies convert this beta-carotene into vitamin A, which plays an important role in supporting our immune system, heart function and good eye health.

Terrific tacos

SERVES 2

Regular readers will know by now that, when it comes to food, my love for all things Mexican knows no bounds! These tacos are really versatile in that you can swap out the steak for a different type of meat such as grilled chicken or pork. Give them a go and I guarantee they'll become a firm favourite.

1 tablespoon extra-virgin olive oil, coconut oil or butter
1 x 300 g minute steak
½ red onion, finely diced
1–2 garlic cloves, finely chopped
1 long red chilli, finely chopped
4 eggs, beaten
1 avocado, sliced
2 large handfuls of coriander sprigs
sea salt

Soft tacos
2 large eggs, beaten
250 ml (1 cup) coconut milk
125 g (1 cup) arrowroot or tapioca flour
3 tablespoons coconut flour
½ teaspoon sea salt
2–3 tablespoons extra-virgin olive oil, coconut oil or butter

To make the tacos, whisk together all the ingredients except the oil or butter in a bowl to form a smooth batter.

Heat a little of the oil or butter in a frying pan over medium heat. Pour 80 ml of the mixture into the frying pan, then tilt and swirl the pan to spread the batter into a 15 cm circle. Reduce the heat to low and cook for 1–2 minutes until sturdy enough to flip, then cook for 1–2 minutes on the other side until cooked through, puffed up and golden brown. Transfer the cooked taco to a plate and repeat this process, adding a little more oil each time, to make six soft tacos.

Heat the oil or butter in a frying pan over medium–high heat. Add the steak and cook for 1 minute on each side, then remove from the pan and wrap in foil for 10 minutes to rest before cutting into thick strips.

Reduce the heat to medium, add the red onion, garlic and chilli to the pan and saute in the steak juices for 2–3 minutes, or until softened and caramelised. Pour over the egg and cook, gently folding the mixture as you go, until scrambled to your liking.

Divide the tacos between plates and top with the scrambled egg, steak strips and avocado slices. Scatter over the coriander and season with salt. Serve.

TIP

To turn these tacos into a delicious burrito, simply pour 250 ml (1 cup) of the batter into a large frying pan and tilt it to spread the batter to the edge of the pan before cooking and topping as per the instructions above (this will make two burritos). Wrap the sides up to form a parcel, then dig in!

Naked lamb burgers

SERVES 2

I think a burger makes the perfect meal no matter what the time of day. I recommend lamb mince here because it's really juicy and flavoursome. The crispy lettuce cups and fresh vegetables help cut through the lamb's natural fattiness really nicely.

400 g lamb mince
2 tablespoons finely chopped
   mint leaves
2 tablespoons finely chopped
   flat-leaf parsley leaves
1 teaspoon onion powder
1 teaspoon garlic powder
1 teaspoon ground cumin
1 teaspoon ground coriander
zest and juice of 1 lemon
sea salt and freshly ground
   black pepper
1 tablespoon extra-virgin olive oil,
   coconut oil or butter

To serve
a few iceberg, gem or cos
   lettuce leaves
2 tablespoons Zucchini Hummus
   (see page 76)
½ tomato, finely sliced
1 beetroot, grated
2 fried eggs
½ avocado, sliced

To make the lamb patties, add the mince, herbs, powdered onion and garlic, spices and lemon zest and juice to a large bowl. Using your hands, mix everything together really well so that the flavourings are evenly distributed through the mince. Season the mixture well with salt and pepper, then shape into two even patties.

Melt the oil or butter in a large frying pan over medium heat, add the patties and fry for 3–4 minutes on each side, or until just cooked through but still a little pink in the middle. Remove from the pan and set aside on paper towel.

Pile a few lettuce leaves inside each other to create two lettuce cups. Add the patties, zucchini hummus, sliced tomato and grated beetroot. Top with a fried egg and serve with slices of avocado on the side.

THE LOWDOWN

Did you know that, just like oily fish, lamb is a great source of healthy omega-3 fatty acids? It also contains high levels of iron, which both our immune and nervous systems need to function properly.

VEGETABLES

Golden cauliflower

SERVES 4–6

Turmeric has certainly taken off in popularity of late, and for good reason – it is packed with health benefits including powerful anti-inflammatory properties. As turmeric is fat-soluble, we need to pair it with a good-quality fat source to absorb its goodness, which is why this recipe celebrates butter in all its delicious glory! This is one of those recipes that really impresses when it lands on the table; it is visually exciting and vibrant, with flavour and health benefits to match!

1 large head of cauliflower
120 g butter, melted
3 tablespoons coconut milk
1 tablespoon ground turmeric
1 tablespoon ground cumin
1 tablespoon ground coriander
1 teaspoon chilli powder
zest and juice of 1 lime
3 tablespoons flat-leaf parsley
  leaves

Mustard butter
40 g butter, softened
1 tablespoon dijon mustard
zest and juice of 1 lemon
sea salt

Preheat the oven to 220°C and line a baking tray with baking paper.

Trim the base of the cauliflower, removing the woody stem and any green leaves. Blanch in a large saucepan of salted boiling water for 3 minutes, then remove and set aside.

To make the mustard butter, whisk the ingredients together in a bowl. Transfer to the fridge to chill and firm.

In a large bowl, combine the melted butter, coconut milk, turmeric, cumin, coriander, chilli powder and lime zest and juice. Holding the cauliflower by its base, dunk it into the bowl, using your hands to ensure the entire head is coated in the mixture. Place the cauliflower on the prepared baking tray and bake for 40–50 minutes, or until golden brown on top and soft in the centre when pierced with the point of a sharp knife.

Remove the baked cauliflower from the oven and leave to cool slightly before cutting into wedges. Serve topped with the mustard butter and chopped flat-leaf parsley.

THE LOWDOWN

I always use grass-fed butter in my cooking, as analysis has shown that only butter from grass-fed cows contains high amounts of fat-soluble vitamins A, D, K and E, as well as their naturally occurring cofactors to absorb them.

Coconut-glazed eggplant

SERVES 4

This is my take on the well-known Japanese eggplant dish nasu dengaku. In my version, the delicious, tender oven-baked eggplant slices are brushed with a sweet coconut aminos glaze, offering you a soy-free alternative to the original.

8 Japanese eggplants (about 600 g)
3 tablespoons coconut oil, melted
sea salt
½ daikon, julienned
1 tablespoon white sesame seeds
1 tablespoon poppy seeds
mint leaves, to serve

Coconut glaze
3 tablespoons coconut aminos
1 tablespoon sugar-free fish sauce
1 teaspoon finely grated ginger

Preheat the oven to 180°C and line a baking tray with baking paper.

For the glaze, mix all the ingredients in a small bowl.

Cut the eggplants in half lengthways, then using a sharp knife score the flesh side and brush with the melted coconut oil to coat. Season with salt and place on the prepared baking tray, cut-side up.

Cook for 6–8 minutes, or until lightly golden, then brush the scored eggplant flesh generously with the glaze and cook for a further 6–8 minutes, or until nicely softened and cooked through. Divide among plates, top with the daikon and scatter over the poppy seeds and mint. Serve.

TIP

The long thin eggplants used in this dish are actually claimed by two countries – Japan and Lebanon. They can be found in most Asian supermarkets or farmers' markets. If you can't get your hands on any, you can use regular eggplants – just increase the cooking time by a few minutes to ensure they are cooked all the way through.

THE LOWDOWN

Daikon is fantastic for promoting good digestive health, as it helps to prevent constipation and improves our gut's ability to absorb the nutrients from the food we eat – enabling us to get the most out of all those wonderful good-quality proteins, smart carbs and healthy fats that we look to celebrate in our diets. Remember, it's not just about what we eat, but also what we absorb!

Cauliflower nuggets with spicy sriracha dipping sauce (LC) (S)

SERVES 4

I love these little crunchy, low-carb morsels but that shouldn't come as a surprise, as I'm a sucker for anything small, fried and crispy. Together with this spicy sriracha sauce they make for perfect couch food – just put on a good movie and get dipping!

2 eggs
100 g (1 cup) almond meal
2 tablespoons sesame seeds
1 tablespoon smoked paprika
sea salt
1 large head of cauliflower,
  broken into florets
150 g (½ cup) Mayo
  (see page 262)
1 tablespoon coconut
  aminos

Sriracha sauce
300 g bird's eye or jalapeño
  chillies, roughly chopped
4 garlic cloves
1½ tablespoons apple cider
  vinegar
1½ tablespoons tomato paste
1 tablespoon honey or pure
  maple syrup
1 tablespoons sugar-free
  fish sauce
½ teaspoon sea salt

For the sriracha sauce, place all the ingredients in a food processor or blender and blitz until completely smooth. Transfer the mixture to a saucepan and bring to the boil, then reduce the heat to low and simmer for 5–10 minutes, or until thickened and reduced by one third. Season to taste, then remove from the heat and leave to cool.

Preheat the oven to 200°C and line a baking tray with baking paper.

Lightly beat the eggs in a shallow bowl. In a separate shallow bowl, mix the almond meal, sesame seeds, paprika and 1 teaspoon of salt.

Dip a cauliflower floret briefly into the beaten egg and shake off any excess, then dip into the almond meal mixture to coat evenly. Transfer to the prepared baking tray and repeat with the rest of the florets. Bake for 15–20 minutes, or until golden brown and crispy.

While the florets are baking, make the dipping sauce by combining 2 tablespoons of the sriracha with the mayo and coconut aminos in a bowl.

Remove the crispy cauliflower florets from the oven and season with a little extra salt to taste. Serve alongside the dipping sauce.

TIPS

Leftover sriracha sauce will keep stored in an airtight container in the fridge for up to 1 week. I love it served with grilled meats, dolloped over a burger or even used to coat veggies before chargrilling for extra flavour.

To make this recipe nut free, simply swap out the almond meal used in the coating for coconut flour.

Abundance bowl

SERVES 2

If you're looking for ways to get more vegetables into your life then look no further than this rainbow bowl. Colourful, vibrant and packed with flavour and nutrition, it's also really versatile when it comes to swapping out the veg for whatever you might have to hand: carrot, kohlrabi, chard . . . the list is endless. So, what are you waiting for – it's time to get creative!

Roast pumpkin
½ small butternut pumpkin, peeled and cut into 2 cm cubes
½ teaspoon smoked paprika
1 teaspoon extra-virgin olive oil

Zesty slaw
½ fennel bulb, finely sliced
⅛ red cabbage, finely sliced
⅛ green cabbage, finely sliced
zest and juice of 1 lemon

Kale and spinach
2 large handfuls of kale, stalks removed, leaves roughly chopped
2 large handfuls of English spinach, stalks removed, leaves roughly chopped
2 tablespoons extra-virgin olive oil
pinch of sea salt

Spiced cauliflower rice
1 tablespoon extra-virgin olive oil
400 g (2 cups) Cauliflower Rice (see page 262)
1 teaspoon ground turmeric
1 teaspoon ground cumin

Green avocado salsa
1 Lebanese cucumber, cut into 1 cm cubes
1 avocado, cut into 2 cm cubes
1 tablespoon extra-virgin olive oil

Beetroot–yoghurt dressing
250 g (1 cup) coconut yoghurt
1 large beetroot, grated
2 tablespoons extra-virgin olive oil
zest and juice of 1 lemon
sea salt and freshly ground black pepper

To serve
3 tablespoons roughly chopped roasted almonds
2 tablespoons white sesame seeds

Preheat the oven to 220°C and line a baking tray with baking paper.

For the roast pumpkin, add the pumpkin, paprika and oil to a bowl and mix together well to coat. Arrange the pumpkin on the prepared baking tray in an even layer and roast for 20 minutes, or until tender.

To make the slaw, toss together all the ingredients in a bowl.

For the kale and spinach, add all the ingredients to a bowl and, using your hands, massage the oil into the leaves to soften.

To make the spiced cauliflower rice, heat the oil in a frying pan over high heat. Add the cauliflower rice, turmeric and cumin, stirring well to coat the cauliflower pieces. Cook for 3–4 minutes, or until warmed through, then remove from the heat and set aside.

For the green avocado salsa, toss together all the ingredients in a bowl.

For the beetroot–yoghurt dressing, place all the ingredients except the salt and pepper in a food processor and blitz until smooth and creamy. Season with salt and pepper to taste.

To build your bowls, pile up the different components in separate areas of your bowls. Drizzle over a little of the beetroot yoghurt dressing and scatter over some chopped roasted almonds and sesame seeds to serve.

TIPS

To save time here you can finely slice the cabbage and fennel for the slaw using a food processor with the slicer attachment added.

Any dressing not used in this dish can be stored in an airtight container in the fridge for up to 7 days. It's great dolloped over my lamb burgers (see page 83).

Charred veggie salad with sensational sour cream Ⓢ Ⓥ

SERVES 2

A celebration of all those lovely, smoky, caramelised flavours that chargrilling brings out in vegetables, this salad is a real winner – especially when topped with generous dollops of my sensational macadamia sour cream.

1 long sweet potato, cut lengthways into 5 mm thick slices
2 Hungarian peppers or green capsicums, quartered or thickly sliced
8 brussels sprouts, trimmed and halved
2 zucchini, cut lengthways into 5 mm thick slices
1 teaspoon ground cumin
1 teaspoon ground turmeric
3 tablespoons extra-virgin olive oil
sea salt and freshly ground black pepper

Dressing
3 tablespoons extra-virgin olive oil
2 tablespoons apple cider vinegar
1 tablespoon pure maple syrup
3 large handfuls of flat-leaf parsley leaves, finely chopped

Macadamia sour cream
160 g (1 cup) macadamia or cashew nuts, soaked in water for 3 hours
zest and juice of 1 lemon
80 ml (⅓ cup) filtered water

To make the macadamia sour cream, add the ingredients to a food processor and blitz until smooth and creamy. Set aside.

Heat a barbecue or large chargrill pan to medium.

In a large bowl, combine the sweet potato, pepper or capsicum, brussels sprouts, zucchini, cumin, turmeric and olive oil. Mix together well and season with salt and pepper to taste.

Add the sweet potato, pepper or capsicum and brussels sprout pieces to the barbecue grill or chargrill pan and cook for 10–12 minutes, turning them halfway, until softened and charred. Remove from the heat and set aside on a serving platter, then add the zucchini to the grill and cook for 1–2 minutes on each side, being careful not to overcook it. Remove from the heat and set aside with the rest of the veg.

Whisk all the dressing ingredients together in a bowl to combine, then pour over the chargrilled vegetables and toss together to coat. Serve with generous dollops of the macadamia sour cream.

TIP

Leftover sour cream can be kept in an airtight container in the fridge for up to 3 days. It makes a delicious extra topping for my chicken nachos (see page 173).

THE LOWDOWN

Macadamias are by far my favourite nut! They are packed full of omega-3 fatty acids, which help support healthy brain function and hormone balance as well as being an essential source of fuel for those on a reduced-carb approach. Plus, they're rich, buttery and creamy – the perfect combo for whipping up dairy-free alternatives to some of your favourite sauces, cheeses and dressings.

Crispy cauliflower steaks with beetroot hummus and pine nut dukkah (K) (LC) (S) (V)

SERVES 4

To me, this recipe is the perfect combination of flavours, colours and textures. This bright and uplifting plate of goodness offers a deliciously charred caramelised flavour from the cauliflower, served on the most addictive beetroot hummus and topped with a pine nut dukkah that gives the most incredible crunch. I think you're really going to enjoy this one, guys!

1 large head of cauliflower
2 tablespoons extra-virgin olive
  oil, coconut oil or butter
sea salt and freshly ground
  black pepper
1 tablespoon dried chilli flakes
juice of 1 lemon

Beetroot hummus
250 ml (1 cup) tahini
250 ml (1 cup) coconut cream
140 g (1 cup) grated beetroot
2 tablespoons olive oil
zest and juice of 1 lemon
1 garlic clove, peeled

Pine nut dukkah
80 g (½ cup) pine nuts
80 g (½ cup) sesame seeds
1 teaspoon ground coriander
½ teaspoon ground cumin
¼ teaspoon ground cinnamon
¼ teaspoon chilli powder
¼ teaspoon ground nutmeg
½ teaspoon sea salt

Preheat the oven to 180°C and line a baking tray with baking paper.

Sit the cauliflower upright on your chopping board and cut four even slices about 4 cm thick out of the centre, reserving the outer pieces for another meal (see tip).

Heat the oil or butter in a frying pan over high heat. Add one of the cauliflower steaks to the pan and fry for 4 minutes, turning halfway through, or until nicely caramelised. Transfer the caramelised steak to the prepared baking tray and repeat with the remaining cauliflower steaks.

Season the cauliflower steaks well with salt and pepper and scatter over the chilli flakes, then roast in the oven for 20–30 minutes, or until cooked through and soft on the inside and golden brown on the edges.

Meanwhile, to make the beetroot hummus, place all the ingredients in a food processor and blend until smooth.

For the dukkah, toast the pine nuts and sesame seeds in a dry frying pan over medium heat until just starting to colour, then add the remaining ingredients and toast, stirring, until golden (the nuts can burn easily, so keep a close eye on them as you go). Transfer to a bowl and set aside.

To serve, spread a generous smear of the beetroot hummus over each serving plate in a circular pattern. Top with the cauliflower steaks, squeeze over the lemon juice and finish with a generous sprinkling of the pine nut dukkah. Enjoy.

TIP

The cauliflower offcuts can be saved to make another delicious meal during the week or added to your next batch of cauliflower rice (see page 262).

Slow-cooked veggie curry

SERVES 4

Often when I think of curries, I imagine the protein being the hero of the dish, with some vegetables to add flavour and texture. I really wanted to flip this notion on its head and show that you can have a curry where vegetables are the true hero. Of course, you can add an animal protein if you wish, but I do think this slow-cooked curry really packs a punch when you're looking for some warmth and nourishment on your plate.

2 tablespoons coconut oil, butter or ghee
1 brown onion, roughly chopped
2 garlic cloves, roughly chopped
250 ml (1 cup) coconut cream
1 tablespoon ground cumin
1 tablespoon ground coriander
1 tablespoon ground turmeric (or a 1 cm piece of fresh turmeric, peeled and finely grated)
1 teaspoon garam masala
1 teaspoon ground ginger
1 butternut pumpkin, peeled and cut into 4 cm chunks
250 ml (1 cup) vegetable stock
1 head of broccoli, broken into small florets
1 head of cauliflower, broken into small florets
1 red capsicum, deseeded and sliced
1 green capsicum, deseeded and sliced
100 g brussels sprouts, trimmed and quartered
4 tomatoes, roughly chopped
75 g (½ cup) cashew nuts, roughly chopped
200 g baby spinach leaves
sea salt and freshly ground black pepper

To serve
finely chopped coriander leaves
chopped toasted cashew nuts
Cauliflower Rice (see page 262) (optional)

Melt the oil, butter or ghee in a large frying pan over medium heat, add the onion and garlic and saute for 3–4 minutes, or until softened and starting to caramelise.

Pour in the coconut cream, stir in the ground spices and bring to a simmer, then add the pumpkin and cook, stirring occasionally, for 10–12 minutes, or until the liquid has thickened and reduced and the pumpkin has softened. Add the stock and remaining vegetables except the spinach and cook for a further 10 minutes, or until the vegetables are tender and the sauce is lovely and thick. Stir through the cashew nuts and baby spinach leaves and cook for another 1–2 minutes, or until the spinach has wilted, then season with salt and pepper to taste and remove from the heat.

To serve, spoon the curry into bowls, scatter over a little chopped coriander and some chopped toasted cashew nuts. Accompany with cauliflower rice, if you like.

Note: to up the carbs here, simply swap out the pumpkin for sweet potato and/or carrots. Conversely, to make this curry keto, simply remove the pumpkin and add extra cauliflower as a replacement.

Best baked butternut

SERVES 2

I feel like something of a late bloomer when it comes to celebrating pumpkin, as for so long in my life it has played second fiddle to sweet potato. What I particularly love about pumpkin is that it's naturally sweet when oven-roasted, while it's still a great lower-carb vegetable option. It's hearty, fulfilling and nourishing: what more could you ask for in a humble vegetable?

310 ml (1¼ cups) filtered water
200 g (1 cup) red quinoa, rinsed
sea salt
1 small butternut pumpkin, halved lengthways and seeds removed
3 tablespoons extra-virgin olive oil
1 small red onion, finely chopped
1 long red chilli, finely chopped
3 tablespoons finely chopped flat-leaf parsley
2 garlic cloves, very finely chopped
2 teaspoons ground cumin
2 teaspoons ground coriander
freshly ground black pepper

To serve
2 tablespoons pine nuts, toasted
2 tablespoons pumpkin seeds, toasted
2 teaspoons dried chilli flakes

Bring the water to the boil in a medium–large saucepan. Add the quinoa and a generous pinch of salt. Return to the boil then immediately cover with a lid, reduce the heat to the lowest setting possible and simmer gently for 15 minutes. During this time, do not stir or move the quinoa in any way.

Remove the pan from the heat and let stand, still with the lid on, for up to 5 minutes. Remove the lid, gently fluff up the grains with a fork and set aside to cool.

Preheat the oven to 200°C and line a baking tray with baking paper.

Using a spoon, scoop out and reserve 4–6 tablespoons of flesh from the pumpkin halves to make room for the filling. Brush the pumpkin halves with 1½ tablespoons of the olive oil to coat evenly.

Grate the reserved pumpkin flesh and transfer to a large bowl. Add 1 cup of the cooled quinoa (save the leftovers for another salad) together with the red onion, chilli, parsley, garlic and ground spices. Season well with salt and pepper and mix to combine.

Add the stuffing mixture to the hollowed-out cavities of the pumpkin halves, using your hands to press it in firmly. Place the pumpkin halves, skin-side down, on the prepared baking tray and drizzle over the remaining olive oil, then cover with foil and bake for 30–40 minutes, until the pumpkin is soft and tender. Divide between plates and serve topped with the toasted pine nuts, pumpkin seeds and chilli flakes.

Okonomiyaki (LC) (S) (NF)

SERVES 2 (MAKES 6 SMALL PANCAKES)

Okonomiyaki is a savoury Japanese pancake containing a variety of delicious and nutrient-rich ingredients. The name is actually derived from the words 'okonomi', meaning 'how you like' and 'yaki', meaning 'grill'. To keep things simple, I suggest using a regular frying pan for this dish, as you'll get all of the fantastic flavours without adding to the washing up!

3 tablespoons coconut oil or extra-virgin olive oil
3 streaky bacon rashers, roughly diced
¼ head of cabbage, shredded
3–4 tablespoons coconut flour, plus extra if needed
½ teaspoon garlic powder
½ teaspoon onion powder
¼ teaspoon sea salt
4 eggs, beaten
2 teaspoons coconut aminos
1 tablespoon sugar-free barbecue sauce
2 tablespoons Mayo (see page 262)
2 spring onions, finely sliced on an angle
1 teaspoon sesame seeds

Heat 1 tablespoon of the oil in a frying pan over medium heat. Add the bacon and fry until nice and crispy, about 5–6 minutes. Remove from the pan and set aside to cool, then transfer to a large bowl.

Add the cabbage, coconut flour, garlic powder, onion powder and salt to the bowl with the bacon and mix well to combine.

In a separate bowl, whisk together the egg and coconut aminos. Pour the egg mixture over the cabbage mix and stir together to form a thick batter, adding a little extra coconut flour if it seems a bit runny.

Preheat the oven to 90°C.

Add another tablespoon of the oil to the frying pan and melt over medium heat. Drop 2 tablespoons of the okonomiyaki batter into the pan and spread gently with the back of a spoon, then repeat twice more to make a batch of even-sized pancakes. Cook for 4–5 minutes, or until golden brown and firm, then use a spatula to flip them over and cook for a further 2–3 minutes on the other side until cooked through. Remove from the pan and keep warm in a low oven. Repeat with the remaining batter, adding another tablespoon of oil to the pan to ensure the pancakes don't stick to it.

Divide the pancakes between plates, drizzle over the barbecue sauce, dollop on the mayonnaise and sprinkle over the spring onion and sesame seeds. Serve.

Saigon sensations (LC) (S) (NF)

SERVES 2

I love creating healthy versions of international classics – the foods that people encounter when travelling or dining at special restaurants, which they can then recreate at home with a healthy twist. These 'Saigon sensations' are my take on the well-known Vietnamese pancakes banh xeo. If you haven't had them before, don't be fooled – while they might be called pancakes they are far from sweet. In Vietnamese, banh xeo means 'sizzling cake' for the sound the batter makes when added to the hot pan, and these nourishing little delights are eaten at any time of day.

4 large eggs, beaten
125 ml (½ cup) coconut milk
1 tablespoon coconut flour
1 teaspoon coconut oil, melted, plus extra for cooking
1 teaspoon ground turmeric
1 teaspoon gluten-free baking powder
pinch of sea salt
lime halves, to serve

Prawn and pork salad
2 tablespoons coconut oil
½ brown onion, finely diced
1 garlic clove, very finely chopped
1 long red chilli, finely chopped
200 g pork mince
sea salt and freshly ground black pepper
100 g large raw prawns, shelled, deveined and roughly chopped into large chunks
80 g bean sprouts
1 large handful of mixed Asian herbs (coriander, Vietnamese mint or Thai basil)

Nuoc cham (Vietnamese chilli dressing)
zest and juice of 2 limes
3 tablespoons sugar-free fish sauce
1 tablespoon filtered water
1 teaspoon coconut sugar
1 teaspoon coconut aminos
1 long red chilli, deseeded and finely chopped
1 garlic clove, finely chopped

In a bowl, whisk the egg, coconut milk, coconut flour, coconut oil, turmeric, baking powder and salt to form a batter. Set aside.

Preheat the oven to 90°C.

To make the nuoc cham, combine all the ingredients in a small bowl and stir together until the sugar has dissolved. Set aside.

For the prawn and pork salad, melt 1 tablespoon of the coconut oil in a non-stick frying pan over high heat. Add the onion, garlic, chilli and pork mince and stir-fry for 5 minutes, or until the onion has softened and the mince is browned and cooked through. Remove from the pan, season with salt and pepper and keep warm in a low oven.

Melt the remaining coconut oil in the same pan, then add the prawns and cook, stirring occasionally, for 2–3 minutes, or until golden and cooked through. Remove from the pan, season with salt and pepper and keep warm in the oven with the mince.

Now let's get onto the pancakes. Set the pan over medium–high heat and lightly grease with a little extra coconut oil if needed. Ladle half the pancake batter into the pan and carefully tilt the pan, swirling the batter to cover the base and reach slightly up the side. Cook for 2–3 minutes, or until the underside is firm and lightly golden, then carefully flip over with a spatula and cook for a further 30 seconds. Transfer the pancake to a plate and repeat with the remaining batter.

To construct the salad, toss the warm pork mince and prawns together with the bean sprouts and Asian herbs in a bowl.

Divide the pancakes between two plates and top with the salad. Pour over the nuoc cham and serve with lime halves for squeezing over. Dig in.

Indian-spiced brussels with smoky mayo (K) (LC) (S)

SERVES 4

I adore both Indian and Mexican food and find it hard to decide which is my favourite – I think the reason I love them both so much is their use of vibrant spices and fresh ingredients, not to mention lots of lovely heat from those chillies! These Indian-spiced brussels are deep-fried in coconut oil for super-crispy results and take the veg to the next level, especially when dipped in my awesome smoky mayo.

coconut oil, for deep-frying
800 g brussels sprouts, trimmed
  and halved
2 sprigs curry leaves
sea salt and freshly ground
  black pepper

Smoky mayo
2 teaspoons smoked paprika
1 teaspoon chilli powder
150 g (½ cup) Mayo (see
  page 262)

To make the smoky mayo, stir the paprika and chilli powder through the mayo in a small bowl. Set aside.

Half-fill a large heavy-based saucepan with coconut oil over medium heat. Heat the oil to 180°C. (To test if the oil is hot enough, simply drop a brussels leaf into the oil – if it sizzles and bubbles, you're good to go.)

Carefully lower the brussels into the hot oil in small batches and cook for 3–4 minutes, or until golden brown and crisp on all sides. Remove from the pan using a slotted spoon and transfer to a plate lined with paper towel to drain. Repeat with the remaining brussels, being sure to bring the oil back up to heat between batches. Transfer to a serving bowl.

Add the curry leaves to the oil for just a few seconds to crisp up, then remove with a slotted spoon and drain on paper towel.

To serve, toss the crispy curry leaves together with the brussels sprouts, season with salt and pepper to taste and serve immediately with the smoky mayo for dipping.

THE LOWDOWN

Fresh curry leaves can be found at good fruit and veg stores and most Asian supermarkets. They bring an awesome number of health benefits that include helping to improve heart function and strengthen our immune systems, as well as increasing the vitality and condition of our hair and skin.

'Tater tots' Ⓢ Ⓥ

SERVES 4

For the uninitiated, tater tots are small, cylindrical deep-fried potato pieces. Coated in a processed gluten-based batter and made with high-starch white potato, the typical variety might be off limits for those of us following a lower-carb, primal diet, but that's no problem here – this sweet potato and pumpkin version with its crispy paleo batter is out of this world.

extra-virgin olive oil, coconut oil or butter, to grease
3 small sweet potatoes (about 400 g), peeled and finely diced
450 g pumpkin, peeled and finely diced
3 tablespoons coconut flour
1 tablespoon onion flakes
1 tablespoon smoked paprika
2 teaspoons sea salt
2 tablespoons almond meal
2 tablespoons arrowroot or tapioca flour
Smoky Mayo (see page 109), to serve (optional)

Preheat the oven to 180°C. Line a baking tray with baking paper and grease well with oil or butter.

Arrange the sweet potato and pumpkin pieces in a roasting tin and bake for 15–20 minutes, or until soft and tender when pressed with a fork. Remove from the oven and set aside to cool.

Transfer the cooked sweet potato and pumpkin to a food processor and blitz to a puree. Add the coconut flour, onion flakes, paprika and 1 teaspoon of the salt and blitz again to combine.

In a bowl, mix together the almond meal, arrowroot or tapioca flour and remaining teaspoon of salt until the mixture resembles breadcrumbs.

Roll a tablespoon of the sweet potato and pumpkin mixture into an oblong shape, then toss to coat in the almond meal mixture. Transfer to the prepared baking tray and repeat with the rest of the sweet potato and pumpkin mixture.

Bake for 30 minutes or until the tater tots are golden brown on the outside and cooked through in the centre. Serve immediately either on their own or dipped into my delicious smoky mayo.

Fully loaded sweet potato skins with cashew cream (S) (V)

SERVES 4

Sweet potato gets a bit of a workout for those avoiding bread, rice and pasta as sources of carbohydrate, but there's a good reason for this as it's packed with nutrients and flavour. Where I can I like to mix things up and look past the usual mash, fritters and fries – cue these fully loaded sweet potato skins for an epic way to eat this popular veg with a twist.

2 medium–large sweet potatoes, skins scrubbed and dried
2 tablespoons coconut oil
sea salt
½ red onion, finely diced
1 garlic clove, very finely chopped
1 long red chilli, finely chopped
1 teaspoon garam masala
1 teaspoon ground ginger
½ teaspoon cayenne pepper
2 large handfuls of baby spinach leaves, roughly chopped
3 tablespoons finely chopped coriander or flat-leaf parsley
juice of 1 lemon, plus extra to serve

Cashew cream
80 g (½ cup) cashew nuts
125 ml (½ cup) coconut cream
½ teaspoon cayenne pepper
½ teaspoon sea salt
zest and juice of 1 lemon

Preheat the oven to 220°C and line a baking tray with baking paper.

Rub the sweet potatoes with 1 tablespoon of the coconut oil, season with salt and place on the prepared baking tray. Bake for 40 minutes, or until soft when pierced with a fork.

Meanwhile, heat the remaining tablespoon of coconut oil in a saucepan over medium heat. Add the onion, garlic and chilli and saute for 3–4 minutes, or until softened and caramelised, then season with salt and saute for a further 4–5 minutes, until the onion is translucent. Stir in the garam masala, ginger and cayenne pepper to coat, add the chopped spinach and cook, stirring, for 1–2 minutes, until the spinach has wilted. Add the coriander or parsley and lemon juice and give everything a good stir, then remove from the heat and set aside.

Cut the cooked sweet potatoes in half lengthways, scoop out roughly half the flesh into a bowl and roughly mash. Add the spinach, onion and garlic mixture and mix well, then spoon the filling back into the hollowed out sweet potato halves. Transfer the stuffed sweet potato skins to the baking tray and bake for 15–20 minutes, or until the skins start to crisp up and the stuffing is golden brown around the edges.

While the sweet potato skins are baking, make the cashew cream by adding all the ingredients to a food processor and blitzing together until smooth and creamy.

Remove the sweet potato halves from the oven, divide among plates and spoon over a little of the cashew cream. Serve straight away with a squeeze of lemon.

TIP

Leftover cashew cream can be kept in an airtight container in the fridge for up to 5 days – try it spread on a slice of your favourite paleo loaf, dolloped over a burger or added to your favourite Mexican dishes.

Charred broccoli salad Ⓚ Ⓛ🄲 Ⓢ Ⓥ

SERVES 4-6

I absolutely love the flavour of broccoli when it's prepared like this – charring it on the edges while still keeping it slightly crunchy really allows it to show off another side of itself. My tip is to keep a little of the stalk on the broccoli heads before cutting them into slices – this helps to keep the slices intact, making for much easier handling on the grill. This salad is awesome either on its own or as a side.

2 small heads of broccoli, stalks trimmed
1 tablespoon coconut oil or butter, softened
2 lemons, cut into cheeks
125 ml (½ cup) extra-virgin olive oil
2 tablespoons apple cider vinegar, or to taste
1 garlic clove, finely sliced
sea salt and freshly ground black pepper
½ red onion, finely sliced
2 large handfuls of mint, roughly chopped
2 large handfuls of flat-leaf parsley leaves, roughly chopped
2 tablespoons slivered pistachios, toasted, chopped

Cashew feta
155 g (1 cup) cashew nuts, soaked in water for at least 3 hours
1 garlic clove, roughly chopped
2 tablespoons extra-virgin olive oil
juice of 1 lemon
sea salt and freshly ground black pepper

To make the cashew feta, drain the soaked nuts and rinse them really well, then transfer to a food processor, along with the garlic, olive oil and lemon juice. Season with salt and pepper and blend until beautifully smooth, adding a dash of water if needed to loosen everything up a little.

Heat a chargrill pan or barbecue grill to medium.

Cut the trimmed broccoli heads into thick chunks. Massage the coconut oil or butter into the broccoli pieces, then transfer them to the hot pan or grill and cook for 6–8 minutes, turning occasionally, until tender and charred around the edges. Set aside on a plate.

Add the lemon cheeks to the pan or grill, flesh-side down, and cook for 4–6 minutes, turning halfway through, until nicely charred on both sides.

Squeeze the juice from one of the charred lemon cheeks into a bowl. Scrape out the lemon flesh from the squeezed cheek with a fork and add it to the bowl together with the olive oil, apple cider vinegar and garlic. Season well with salt and pepper and mix to combine.

Add the broccoli chunks to a large bowl together with the onion, mint, parsley and three-quarters of the dressing. Toss everything together well with your hands, then transfer to a serving platter.

To serve, drizzle the rest of the dressing over the broccoli salad, crumble over one-third of the feta and scatter over the pistachios. Serve with the remaining charred lemon cheeks for squeezing.

TIP

Leftover cashew feta will keep stored in an airtight container in the fridge for up to 7 days and is great tossed through a salad or as a topping for one of my pizzas (see page 169).

The detox chop

SERVES 2

I love eating salads like this – I really enjoy it when the ingredients are chopped super small and mixed together as I can get loads of different flavours into every mouthful, plus everything gets really well coated with the dressing.

100 g mixed baby salad leaves, finely chopped
100 g watercress, finely chopped
4 celery stalks, finely diced
1 green capsicum, deseeded and finely diced
1 Lebanese cucumber, finely diced
½ bunch of flat-leaf parsley leaves, finely chopped
½ bunch of mint leaves, finely chopped
¼ white cabbage, finely chopped
sea salt and freshly ground black pepper
2 tablespoons crushed and toasted pecans or walnuts

Dressing
1 avocado, mashed
3 tablespoons extra-virgin olive oil
2 tablespoons apple cider vinegar
zest and juice of 1 lime
1 teaspoon hot chilli powder
1 cm piece of ginger, grated (optional)
sea salt and freshly ground black pepper

Add all the salad ingredients except the nuts and seasoning to a large serving bowl and toss together well.

For the dressing, whisk together all the ingredients and 2 tablespoons of water in a small bowl until smooth and creamy.

Pour the dressing over the salad and, using your hands, give everything a good mix to ensure all the ingredients are really well coated with the dressing. Season with salt and pepper, divide between plates and sprinkle over the crushed toasted pecans or walnuts to finish. Enjoy.

TIP

To get things really fine, I sometimes cut up the lettuce and herbs in this salad with kitchen scissors.

Caramelised lemon and zucchini with nut crumb

SERVES 2

This has got to be one of my favourite salad recipes because it combines one of my all-time top veggies, the zucchini, with the unique tartness of caramelised lemon. It's a really good example of how simple flavours can be combined to create something really special.

2 large green zucchini
2 large yellow zucchini
1 tablespoon extra-virgin olive oil
1 lemon, finely sliced
1 tablespoon honey or pure
  maple syrup

Nut crumb
2 tablespoons roughly chopped
  walnuts or pecans
2 tablespoons roughly chopped
  almonds
1 tablespoon sesame seeds

Dressing
125 ml (½ cup) extra-virgin olive oil
2 tablespoons lemon juice
2 tablespoons apple cider vinegar
1 teaspoon dried chilli flakes
sea salt and freshly ground
  black pepper

For the nut crumb, lightly toast the nuts and seeds in a dry frying pan over medium heat for 2–3 minutes, or until golden brown and aromatic. Set aside in a bowl.

Using a mandoline, vegetable peeler or a sharp knife, slice the zucchini into long ribbons and add them to a large bowl.

Heat the olive oil in a large frying pan over medium heat, add the lemon slices and cook for 5–6 minutes, turning halfway through cooking, until softened and caramelised. Drizzle over the honey or maple syrup and cook, stirring to coat, for another 3–4 minutes, or until nice and sticky, then transfer to the bowl with the zucchini. Leave to cool slightly before mixing everything together with your hands.

In a separate bowl, whisk together all the dressing ingredients until well combined. Pour over the salad and toss everything together. Scatter over the nut crumb and give everything a final toss, then serve.

Cauliflower flatbreads with avocado tzatziki (K) (LC) (S) (NF)

SERVES 4

If I haven't already convinced you of how wonderfully versatile cauliflower is when it comes to healthy cooking, these delicious flatbreads should do the job! They're perfect with this avocado tzatziki, but are also pretty great with all of the other healthy dips found in this book.

1 large cauliflower, broken
   into florets
4 eggs
50 g (½ cup) coconut flour
3 tablespoons coconut oil, melted
1 teaspoon ground cumin
1 teaspoon ground coriander
1 teaspoon onion powder
sea salt and freshly ground
   black pepper

Avocado tzatziki
125 g (½ cup) coconut yoghurt
½ cucumber, grated
1 large ripe avocado
1 small garlic clove, grated or
   very finely chopped
2 tablespoons extra-virgin olive oil
1 teaspoon finely chopped dill
   or ¼ teaspoon dried dill
zest and juice of 1 lemon
sea salt and freshly ground
   black pepper

Preheat the oven to 180°C and line a baking tray with baking paper.

Add the cauliflower florets to a steamer or a large saucepan of boiling water and steam or boil until soft, then transfer to a food processor and blitz until smooth.

Add the pureed cauliflower to a large bowl together with the eggs, coconut flour, coconut oil, cumin, coriander and onion powder. Season well with salt and pepper and mix together really well to form a thick batter.

Spoon the mixture onto the prepared baking tray and spread out to an even layer about 5 mm thick. Bake for 25–30 minutes, or until firm to the touch and golden brown.

Meanwhile, make your avocado tzatziki by pulsing together all the ingredients in a food processor to form a chunky paste (if you like it smooth, simply pulse for longer). Set aside.

Remove the flatbread from the oven and cut it into quarters. Carefully flip the pieces over using a spatula, then return the tray to the oven and cook for a further 5 minutes until golden brown.

Cut the flatbreads into your desired shapes and serve with the avocado tzatziki.

Pumpkini slice

SERVES 8-10

If you're short on time but looking for something easy, nutritious and tasty to cook, look no further than this pumpkini slice! It's perfect for making at the start of a busy week and then portioning up for when you're on the move or needing an easy go-to dinner when you get home.

1 tablespoon coconut oil or extra-virgin olive oil

1 small red onion, finely chopped

2 garlic cloves, very finely chopped

1 long red chilli, finely chopped

2 large zucchini, grated

200 g pumpkin, peeled and grated

8 eggs, lightly beaten

125 ml (½ cup) coconut milk

60 g butter, melted, plus extra to serve

100 g (1 cup) almond meal

3 tablespoons chopped flat-leaf parsley leaves

1 teaspoon gluten-free baking powder

sea salt and freshly ground black pepper

Preheat the oven to 180°C and line a 28 x 15 x 7.5 cm loaf tin with baking paper.

Heat the oil in a frying pan over medium heat. Add the onion, garlic and chilli and saute for 3–4 minutes, or until softened and caramelised, then remove from the heat and set aside.

In a bowl, combine the zucchini, pumpkin, egg, coconut milk, butter, almond meal, parsley and baking powder. Season with salt and pepper and mix really well. Add the onion, garlic and chilli and stir to combine.

Spoon the mixture into the prepared loaf tin in an even layer and bake for 30–40 minutes, or until the slice is completely set and golden brown on top.

Remove from the oven and leave to cool slightly before cutting into thick slices. Serve with lashings of butter or toppings of your choice.

TIP

If you've got any leftover cooked protein from other meals, such as shredded chicken, you can always try adding it into the batter before baking in the oven to really jazz it up a little.

FISH & SHELLFISH

Baked salmon with zucchini

SERVES 2

These easy-to-prepare parcels are one of the most delicious ways I know of enjoying salmon. Being fairly firm-fleshed, salmon really lends itself to being cooked in this style as it retains all its moisture, while taking on all the flavours of the other ingredients tucked inside the parcel.

1 lemon
1 yellow zucchini, sliced
   into ribbons
1 green zucchini, sliced
   into ribbons
¼ fennel bulb, finely sliced,
   fronds reserved
8 cherry tomatoes, quartered
12 kalamata olives, pitted and
   halved
2 x 180 g salmon fillets
40 g butter
½ teaspoon smoked paprika
sea salt

Preheat the oven to 180°C and line a baking tray with baking paper. Halve the lemon and cut one of the halves into four thin slices.

Cut out two 30 cm squares of baking paper and lay them out on your work surface. Arrange half the vegetables and olives in the centre of one of the squares to create a bed for a salmon fillet to sit on, then top with the fish and fennel fronds. Place two of the lemon slices on top of the salmon, squeeze over a little lemon juice, top with half the butter and sprinkle over half the smoked paprika. Season with salt, then fold the edges of the baking paper over the salmon to create an enclosed parcel. Secure with cooking twine, then repeat the process with the remaining ingredients.

Transfer the salmon parcels to the prepared baking tray and bake for 8–10 minutes (this will give you salmon that is just cooked but still nicely pink in the middle – leave it for a little longer if you prefer it cooked through). Serve in the paper parcel.

TIP

Sometimes, I roast the zucchini, fennel, olives and cherry tomatoes for a few minutes until lightly caramelised, before dividing them between the paper squares. While it only takes a little bit longer, it gives the veg a really lovely depth of flavour.

That zesty prawn salad (LC) (S)

SERVES 4

Cast your mind back to 2013 and you may remember Scott and I cooking for the first time on My Kitchen Rules. It was a balmy night in Bondi and our entree was our zesty prawn salad. When preparing the dish, we had little idea that it would get us two perfect 10s from Pete and Manu and help us record the highest score in MKR history! Here's the dish Australia fell in love with, just given a little tweak to really celebrate my health philosophy of today.

1 tablespoon extra-virgin olive oil or coconut oil
16 large raw prawns, shelled and deveined
juice of 1 lemon
2 small avocados, cut into 2 cm cubes
2 ruby red grapefruits, segmented and cut into 2 cm cubes
1 long red chilli, finely sliced

Zesty dressing
3 tablespoons lime juice
2 tablespoons coconut sugar
1 tablespoon coconut aminos
2 teaspoons sugar-free fish sauce
½ teaspoon finely grated ginger
1 long red chilli, finely chopped

To serve
Mayo (see page 262) or Tartare (see page 138)
crushed toasted peanuts
Asian micro herbs (such as coriander or shiso)

For the zesty dressing, whisk the ingredients in a bowl until the coconut sugar has dissolved. Set aside.

Heat the oil in a large frying pan over high heat. Add the prawns and cook for 30 seconds or so on each side until coloured and just cooked through. Remove the prawns from the pan and cut them into thirds, then transfer to a large bowl and squeeze over the lemon juice.

Add the avocado, grapefruit and chilli to the bowl, pour over the dressing and toss together well. Serve in wide clear glasses, topped with dollops of mayo or tartare, some crushed toasted peanuts and a scattering of Asian micro herbs.

TIP

This is a great dish for entertaining – try doubling the quantities and serving it in shot glasses as a fresh and zesty canape at your next celebration!

Marrakech skewers

SERVES 4

Marrakech is famous for its vibrant and unique street food. Now, I have spared you healthy recreations of some of the more typical dishes (including snail soup and sheep heads) and kept things nice and simple with these fish skewers. They're a really easy way to discover the amazing flavours Moroccan food has to offer and I think you are going to fall in love with this recipe.

4 x 180 g barramundi fillets, cut into 3.5 cm cubes
2 tablespoons melted butter, coconut oil or extra-virgin olive oil
2 small zucchini, cut into rounds
1 large carrot, cut into ribbons
1 red onion, cut into wedges

Marinade
4 garlic cloves, finely chopped
2 tablespoons finely chopped coriander leaves
2 tablespoons honey or pure maple syrup
3 tablespoons extra-virgin olive oil
½ red onion, roughly diced
½ teaspoon ground coriander
½ teaspoon ground cumin
½ teaspoon hot chilli powder
½ teaspoon ground cinnamon
¼ teaspoon ground allspice
zest and juice of 1 lemon
sea salt and freshly ground black pepper

To serve (optional)
Lemon–Coconut Tahini (see page 133)
Zucchini Hummus (see page 74)

To make the marinade, place all the ingredients in a large bowl and whisk well to combine.

Add the fish pieces to the marinade and toss to coat, then cover with plastic wrap, transfer to the fridge and leave to marinate for 2–3 hours. (Lengthy marinating isn't a deal-breaker here, so if you're short on time you can crack right on with it.)

Preheat a barbecue grill or chargrill pan to medium and brush with the butter or oil.

Thread the marinated barramundi, zucchini, carrot ribbons and onion wedges onto metal skewers in an alternating pattern, folding the carrot ribbons back and forth onto the skewers to press them together.

Grill the skewers for 4–5 minutes on each side, or until the fish is cooked through and the vegetables are tender and caramelised on the edges. Remove from the heat and serve with your favourite condiments, salads and sides (they go well with my lemon coconut tahini and zucchini hummus).

TIP

If you can't source good-quality barramundi or don't live in a region where barra is available, any firm-fleshed white fish will do here – the important thing is that the flesh is firm enough to remain on the skewers during cooking.

Chermoula tiger prawns on lemon–coconut tahini (K) (LC) (S) (NF)

SERVES 4

Prawns are perfectly suited to our Aussie outdoor beach and barbecue culture – they're super easy to cook and pretty much everyone loves them. This simple recipe takes them to the next level by marinating them in chermoula, a traditional Moroccan marinade that is typically used to flavour fish or seafood but is just as delicious slathered over meats or veggies.

1 kg raw tiger prawns, shelled
  with tails left intact, deveined
3 tablespoons extra-virgin olive oil

Chermoula
2 large handfuls of flat-leaf
  parsley leaves, finely chopped
2 large handfuls of coriander
  leaves, finely chopped
2 large handfuls of mint leaves,
  finely chopped
2 garlic cloves, finely chopped
½ red onion, finely chopped
zest and juice of 1 lemon
1 teaspoon ground cumin
3 tablespoons extra-virgin olive oil

Lemon–coconut tahini
250 ml (1 cup) tahini
250 ml (1 cup) coconut cream
1 garlic clove, crushed
zest and juice of 2 lemons
½ teaspoon cayenne paper
½ teaspoon smoked paprika

To serve
basil leaves
lemon rind
extra-virgin olive oil
sea salt

To make the chermoula, combine all the ingredients in a bowl.

Spoon two-thirds of the chermoula into a zip-lock bag, add the prawns, seal and shake well to coat, then transfer to the fridge and leave to marinate for 15 minutes.

Meanwhile, for the lemon–coconut tahini, blend all the ingredients together in a food processor until nice and smooth.

Heat the oil on a barbecue plate over high heat until smoking. Add the prawns and cook for 2 minutes, then turn and cook for a further minute, until the prawns have just changed colour. (You want them to be very slightly underdone at this point as they will continue to cook for a few moments after being removed from the barbecue.)

Generously smear some lemon–coconut tahini on a serving platter and arrange the prawns on top. Scatter over some basil leaves and lemon rind, drizzle with olive oil and season well.

TIPS

Planning to entertain? Pre-marinated prawns are suitable to freeze, meaning you will be good to go the next time you've got guests!

You'll have more lemon–coconut tahini than you need here – store the leftover mix in an airtight container in the fridge for up to 7 days and try serving it with my delicious lamb shoulder (see page 200).

Satay salmon with crunchy cucumber and herb salad (LC) (S)

SERVES 4

It is no secret that I love the flavours of a freshly made satay! Satay, or sate in Indonesian and Malaysian spelling, is a dish of seasoned, skewered and grilled meat, served with a sauce typically made from peanuts. This recipe uses those same flavours but transfers them to salmon fillets, which works really nicely. I've used peanuts in this recipe, but those following a strict paleo approach can always swap them out for cashew nuts instead.

1 x 800 g whole salmon fillet or 4 x 200 g fillets
sea salt and freshly ground black pepper
1 tablespoon coconut oil
½ brown onion, finely chopped
3 garlic cloves, very finely chopped
1 long red chilli, finely chopped
2 tablespoons red curry paste
1 tablespoon coconut aminos or coconut nectar
3 tablespoons peanut butter
1 x 270 ml can coconut milk
3 tablespoons chopped peanuts
3 tablespoons shredded coconut
1 handful of coriander leaves

Cucumber and herb salad
2 continental cucumbers, peeled, seeds removed, thinly sliced
2 large handfuls of coriander leaves, roughly chopped
1 shallot, finely chopped
1 long red chilli, finely chopped
2 tablespoons apple cider vinegar
1 tablespoon coconut aminos or coconut nectar
1 tablespoon sugar-free fish sauce
zest and juice of 1 lime
sea salt and freshly ground black pepper

Preheat the oven to 180°C and line a baking tray with baking paper.

Place the salmon on the prepared baking tray, season well with salt and pepper and bake for 10–12 minutes, or until the flesh is opaque and breaks apart into flakes when pressed with a fork. Cover with foil and set aside to rest.

Meanwhile, heat the coconut oil in a saucepan over medium heat. Add the onion, garlic and chilli and cook, stirring, for 1 minute, then add the curry paste and stir for another minute until you start to smell a lovely aroma as the spices cook off. Add the coconut aminos or nectar, peanut butter and coconut milk to the pan and bring to a simmer, then reduce the heat to low and cook, stirring occasionally, for 6–8 minutes, or until thickened and reduced.

To make the cucumber and herb salad, toss the cucumber, coriander, shallot and chilli together in a bowl. In a separate small bowl, whisk together the apple cider vinegar, coconut aminos or nectar, fish sauce, lime zest and juice. Season the dressing with salt and pepper to taste, then pour over the salad ingredients and toss together well.

Transfer the salmon to a serving platter, spoon over the cucumber and herb salad and sprinkle over the peanuts, shredded coconut and coriander leaves. Serve alongside the warm satay sauce.

Chargrilled octopus with slaw and tartare (LC) (S) (NF)

SERVES 4

I really want to encourage you guys to cook outside of your comfort zone, and part of that means celebrating protein sources you wouldn't normally cook with on a regular basis. For me, one of these ingredients has been octopus, but since I learned to cook it like this I haven't looked back. While it's seriously delicious and also really nutritious, the thing that makes this recipe a real winner is how easy it is to put together. You can easily ask your fishmonger to prepare just the tentacles for you, or simply use the whole octopus as I have here.

1 kg large octopus, whole or just
   tentacles (ask your fishmonger
   to prepare these for you)
2 tablespoons apple cider vinegar
juice of 2 lemons, plus extra
   lemon wedges to serve
125 ml (½ cup) extra-virgin
   olive oil
2 garlic cloves, smashed
2 tablespoons oregano leaves
2 teaspoons sea salt

Cabbage slaw
¼ savoy cabbage, shredded
1 carrot, shredded
3 tablespoons extra-virgin
   olive oil
2 tablespoons apple cider vinegar
1 teaspoon dried chilli flakes
zest and juice of 1 lemon

Tartare
150 g (½ cup) Mayo (see
   page 262)
1 teaspoon apple cider vinegar
1 teaspoon dried dill
1 teaspoon dijon mustard
sea salt and freshly ground
   black pepper

Preheat the oven to 180°C and line a roasting tin with baking paper.

Wash the octopus under cold water and place in the prepared roasting tin with 125 ml (½ cup) water and the apple cider vinegar. Cover the tin with foil – being sure to secure the edges to seal it well – and cook for about 40–45 minutes, or until the octopus is tender when pressed with a fork. Check on it once or twice during this cooking time to ensure it hasn't dried out, adding a dash more water and apple cider vinegar for moisture if necessary.

Transfer the octopus to a large heatproof bowl and add the lemon juice, olive oil, garlic, oregano and salt and mix together well. Cover with plastic wrap and leave to marinate for 30 minutes.

Meanwhile, to make your slaw, combine the cabbage and carrot in a large bowl, add the olive oil, apple cider vinegar, chilli flakes, lemon zest and juice and mix together well with your hands.

To make the tartare, mix all the ingredients in a bowl until well combined.

Heat a chargrill pan or barbecue grill to high. Add the octopus and cook for 3–4 minutes on each side, or until nicely charred and crispy around the edges. Remove from the heat.

Serve the octopus whole on a platter or slice into rough pieces and divide among plates with the cabbage slaw, dollops of the tartare sauce and lemon wedges for squeezing.

Sexy salmon burrito bowl

SERVES 2

Bowls are going off in health circles around the world – pretty much every meal you can imagine is being recreated to suit being eaten in one easy-to-grab-and-go bowl. The phenomenon has really taken over in LA and New York with restaurants there dedicated only to bowl food. There are healthy Indian bowls, smoothie bowls . . . the list is pretty much endless. This sexy salmon burrito bowl is my take.

2 x 200–300 g salmon fillets
2 teaspoons garlic powder
1 teaspoon hot chilli powder
2 teaspoons ground cumin
2 teaspoons ground coriander
½ teaspoon sea salt
1 teaspoon smoked paprika
zest and juice of 1 lime
3 tablespoons extra-virgin olive oil

Lime–coriander cauliflower rice
2 tablespoons coconut oil or
   extra-virgin olive oil
2 garlic cloves, finely chopped
½ brown onion, finely diced
1 long green chilli, finely sliced
400 g (2 cups) Cauliflower Rice
   (see page 262)
zest and juice of 1 lime
sea salt
2 tablespoons finely chopped
   coriander leaves

Caramelised mango
1 mango, cut into cheeks
1 tablespoon coconut oil or
   extra-virgin olive oil

Tomato salsa
2 tomatoes, finely diced
2 tablespoons finely chopped
   coriander
¼ red onion, finely diced
zest and juice of 1 lemon
2 tablespoons extra-virgin olive oil

To serve
8 gem lettuce leaves
1 green capsicum, deseeded
   and finely sliced
2 avocados, sliced
2 lime cheeks

In a large bowl, combine the salmon, garlic and chilli powders, cumin, coriander, salt, paprika, lime zest and juice and 2 tablespoons of the olive oil. Mix well to coat the fish pieces. Transfer to the fridge and leave to marinate for 10–15 minutes.

Heat the remaining 1 tablespoon of olive oil in a frying pan over medium heat. Add the marinated salmon fillets and cook for 5–6 minutes, then turn with tongs and cook for a further 3–4 minutes, or until cooked through. Remove from the heat and set aside to rest.

To make the lime–coriander cauliflower rice, heat the oil in a frying pan over medium–high heat. Add the garlic, onion and chilli and saute for 2–3 minutes, or until softened and caramelised, then add the cauliflower rice, lime zest and juice. Season well with salt and cook, stirring, for 3–4 minutes, or until warmed through. Remove from the heat and set aside. Just before serving, stir through the coriander leaves.

For the caramelised mango, heat a chargrill pan or barbecue grill to high. Brush the mango cheeks generously with oil and cook, flesh-side down, for 3–4 minutes, or until golden brown and charred. Remove from the heat and set aside.

To make the tomato salsa, mix all the ingredients in a bowl.

Now let's assemble these bad boys. Take two shallow bowls and place four lettuce leaves and one of the caramelised mango cheeks in each. Divide the cauliflower rice between the bowls and top with the salmon, then spoon over the salsa. Finally, arrange the capsicum, avocado and lime cheeks around the sides and dig in.

TIP

This bowl is really flexible, with the vibrant Mexican flavours lending themselves to so many fantastic variations. If you want to experiment, start by swapping the salmon out for chilli con carne, grilled chicken or pork fillet and take things from there . . . enjoy!

Crispy skin ocean trout with coconut cauliflower puree and herb butter (K) (LC) (S) (NF)

SERVES 2

I love ocean trout and although it very much resembles salmon in appearance, it tastes pretty different. Don't worry if you can't get hold of any trout; the great thing about this recipe is that the flavour combination works incredibly well with both!

1 tablespoon extra-virgin olive oil, coconut oil or butter
sea salt
2 x 200 g ocean trout fillets, skin on
40 g unsalted butter
1 garlic clove, crushed
2 tablespoons finely chopped flat-leaf parsley leaves
zest and juice of 1 lemon

Coconut cauliflower puree
500 g cauliflower, broken into small florets
1 x 270 ml can coconut cream
250 ml (1 cup) chicken stock
40 g butter, chopped
sea salt

To make the coconut cauliflower puree, add the cauliflower florets, coconut cream and chicken stock to a saucepan and bring to the boil, then reduce the heat to low and simmer, covered, for 15–20 minutes, or until the cauliflower is tender. Drain most of the liquid, keeping 2 tablespoons or so, then transfer the cauliflower and reserved liquid to a food processor with the butter and salt and whiz together until smooth. Return to the pan and keep warm.

Heat the oil or butter in a frying pan over medium heat. Season the fish well on both sides, add it to the pan, skin-side down, and cook for 4–5 minutes, or until the skin is golden brown and crisp. Turn and cook for a further 3–4 minutes, or until cooked through. Remove from the pan and set aside to rest.

Add the butter, garlic and parsley to the pan and cook together with the fish juices for 2–3 minutes to make a lovely herby, buttery sauce. Stir in the lemon zest and juice, then remove from the heat.

To serve, divide the coconut cauliflower puree between plates, lay over the fish fillets and spoon over the herb butter. Enjoy.

THE LOWDOWN

This dish is rich in butter, and for good reason! Butter is a good source of important fat-soluble vitamins A, D, E and K2. These vitamins occur in large amounts only when the butter comes from grass-fed cows.

MEAT & POULTRY

Beef ragu with easy pappardelle

SERVES 4

I first fell in love with ragu at a quaint little restaurant in Bronte, which was famous for its duck ragu with pappardelle. Sadly, the restaurant is no longer there, but my memory of that dish lives on. Here is my version using beef as the protein and parsnips as the pasta – I hope you love it just as much as I loved the original.

2 tablespoons extra-virgin olive oil, coconut oil or butter
800 g stewing steak, chuck steak or rib-eye, cut into rough chunks
sea salt
2 celery stalks, roughly diced
4 garlic gloves, very finely chopped
1 carrot, roughly chopped
1 brown onion, finely chopped
1 long red chilli, roughly chopped
250 ml (1 cup) beef stock or bone broth
1 x 400 g can crushed tomatoes
2 dried bay leaves
2 teaspoons dried basil
1 teaspoon smoked paprika
1 tablespoon coconut aminos
freshly ground black or white pepper
5–6 parsnips

To serve
extra-virgin olive oil
roughly chopped flat-leaf parsley

Heat the oil or butter in a heavy-based saucepan over medium heat. Season the beef generously with salt, then add to the pan and saute for 3–4 minutes, or until sealed and browned on all sides. Remove from the pan and set aside.

Add the celery, garlic, carrot, onion and chilli to the pan and saute for 5–6 minutes, or until softened, caramelised and lightly golden.

Return the beef to the pan and add the stock or broth, crushed tomatoes, bay leaves, basil, paprika, coconut aminos and pepper. Bring to the boil, then reduce the heat to medium–low, cover with a lid and cook for 2 hours, or until the meat is meltingly tender.

While the ragu is cooking, use a mandoline, spiraliser or a sharp knife to slice the parsnips into fine ribbons.

Using two forks, gently shred the meat in the pan, then continue to cook, uncovered and stirring, for 5–10 minutes, or until the ragu has thickened and reduced nicely. Season with salt and pepper to taste. Carefully stir through the parsnip ribbons and cook for a further 2–3 minutes. Divide the ragu among serving plates and serve drizzled with a little extra-virgin olive oil and a sprinkling of chopped parsley.

Note: want to make this recipe keto? Simply swap the parsnips for zucchini noodles and you're good to go!

Moreish meatloaf (LC) (S)

SERVES 6-8

Meatloaf has certainly stood the test of time, standing firm as a family favourite after decades of reinvention, and for good reason – it's easy to make, flexible and good for you. What I mean by flexible is that you can pretty much use whatever mince you've got on hand. It makes a great family feast, as well as being the perfect recipe to make at the beginning of the week and portion out over the following days.

2 tablespoons extra-virgin olive oil
6 streaky bacon rashers, roughly chopped
1 brown onion, diced
1 carrot, grated
4 garlic cloves, finely chopped
2 tablespoons roughly chopped thyme leaves
1 kg pork and veal mince (or any mince you have on hand)
55 g (½ cup) almond meal
125 ml (½ cup) coconut milk
2 eggs
2 tablespoons coconut aminos
2 tablespoons tomato paste
2 teaspoons salt
1 teaspoon freshly ground black pepper
2 x 400 g cans chopped tomatoes
250 ml (1 cup) beef, chicken or vegetable stock

Preheat the oven to 200°C.

Heat the oil in a frying pan over medium–high heat. Add the bacon, onion, carrot, garlic and thyme and saute for 4–5 minutes, or until the onion and garlic are softened and caramelised and the bacon is crispy. Remove from the heat and tip the bacon and onion mixture into a large bowl.

Add the mince, almond meal, coconut milk, eggs, coconut aminos, tomato paste, salt and pepper to the bowl. Using your hands, mix everything together really well so that the flavourings are evenly distributed through the mince.

Pile the mince mixture into the centre of a roasting tin and shape it with your hands into a rough loaf shape. Pour the chopped tomatoes and stock around the meatloaf, then transfer to the oven and bake for 45 minutes, or until the meatloaf is a lovely golden brown and the sauce has thickened and reduced.

Remove from the oven and set aside to cool for 10 minutes before slicing up the meatloaf and dividing among plates. Spoon over the sauce and serve.

TIP

If you are making this meatloaf in advance, store it in an airtight container in the fridge for up to 5 days or in the freezer for up to 3 months, defrosting it in the fridge overnight before reheating.

Lamb moussaka (LC)(S)(NF)

SERVES 4–6

Most of the world thinks of moussaka as a Greek dish, but funnily enough the Greeks believe it was created by the Arabs when they brought the eggplant to Greece. Regardless of who takes ownership of this simple and delicious dish, one thing I know for certain is that you will love this healthy dairy- and gluten-free version.

1 large eggplant (about 500 g), sliced lengthways into 1 cm thick slices
sea salt
80 ml (⅓ cup) extra-virgin olive oil, coconut oil or butter
200 g silverbeet or English spinach, stalks removed and leaves roughly chopped
2 brown onions, roughly chopped
4 garlic cloves, crushed
1 long red chilli, roughly chopped
1 teaspoon ground cinnamon
1 teaspoon ground allspice
700 g lamb mince (the fattier the better)
freshly ground black pepper
3 tablespoons tomato paste
250 ml (1 cup) beef, chicken or vegetable stock
2 large handfuls of flat-leaf parsley leaves, roughly chopped
salad leaves, to serve

Cauliflower sauce
½ head cauliflower, cut into small florets
250 ml (1 cup) coconut milk
1½ tablespoons arrowroot or tapioca flour
1 egg

Season the eggplant slices well with salt on both sides and set aside in a colander for 1 hour to draw out any excess moisture. Rinse under cold water to remove the salt, then pat dry with paper towel.

Heat 1 tablespoon of the oil or butter in a large frying pan over medium–high heat, add one-third of the eggplant slices and fry for 2–3 minutes on each side, or until golden brown. Set aside on a plate and repeat with the remaining eggplant, adding another tablespoon of oil or butter to the pan between each batch.

Add a little more oil or butter to the pan, together with the silverbeet or spinach and saute for 3–4 minutes, or until nicely wilted. Remove from the pan and set aside.

Reduce the heat to medium and add the remaining oil or butter to the pan. Add the onion, garlic, chilli and spices and saute for 4–5 minutes, or until softened and caramelised. Add the lamb mince, breaking it up with the back of a wooden spoon, and cook until evenly brown. Season generously with salt and pepper, add the tomato paste and stock and simmer gently, uncovered, for 15–20 minutes, or until thickened and reduced.

Meanwhile, make the cauliflower sauce. Steam the cauliflower florets for 10–15 minutes, or until lovely and tender. Set aside. Whisk the coconut milk and arrowroot or tapioca flour in a saucepan over medium heat. Bring to the boil, then reduce to a simmer and cook, stirring, for 15–20 minutes, or until thickened. Remove from the heat and beat in the egg, then transfer to a food processor with the cauliflower and blitz until smooth and creamy.

Preheat the oven to 180°C and grease a baking dish with oil.

To assemble your moussaka, lay half the eggplant over the bottom of your prepared baking dish. Cover with the silverbeet or spinach, then spread over the lamb mince and top with the remaining eggplant. Sprinkle over the parsley and pour over the cauliflower sauce.

Bake for 45 minutes or until lightly golden on top, then remove from the oven and set aside for 10 minutes to cool slightly. Serve with a simple salad.

Coconut roast chicken with lime and coriander

SERVES 4

Roast chicken is often paired with familiar ingredients, such as lemon, thyme and roast vegetables. As delicious and perfect as these flavour combos are, I wanted to bring something fresh, summery and tropical to your dining table here. Introducing my coconut roast chicken with lime and coriander – try it and prepare to be transported to a beach in Thailand, with water lapping at your feet and fresh Asian flavours buzzing on your tastebuds after a day in the ocean ...

20 g butter
100 g (½ cup) raw Cauliflower Rice (see page 262)
sea salt
4 garlic cloves, roughly chopped
2 cm piece of ginger, roughly chopped
1 lemongrass stalk, white part only
1 bunch of coriander, stems roughly chopped and leaves reserved
2 kaffir lime leaves, stems removed
zest and juice of 2 limes
60 g (1 cup) shredded or flaked coconut, lightly toasted, plus extra to serve
1 x 1.5 kg whole chicken
500 ml (2 cups) chicken stock
3 tablespoons sugar-free fish sauce
3 tablespoons coconut aminos
lime cheeks, to serve

Preheat the oven to 180°C.

Melt the butter in a frying pan over medium heat, add the cauliflower rice and saute for 3–4 minutes, or until golden brown. Season with salt, remove from the heat and set aside.

Add the garlic, ginger, lemongrass, coriander stems, kaffir lime leaves and the lime zest and juice to a food processor and pulse to form a rough, chunky paste.

Transfer the mixture to a bowl, add the cauliflower rice, coriander leaves and coconut and mix everything together with your hands until well combined. Stuff the mixture into the chicken cavity, then secure the legs with bamboo skewers or kitchen twine.

Pour the stock, fish sauce and coconut aminos into a roasting tin and stir to mix well. Place the chicken, breast-side down, in the tin, then transfer to the oven and roast for 40 minutes, basting with the delicious pan juices at 15-minute intervals. Flip the chicken over and roast, basting again every 15 minutes, for another 40 minutes, or until the juices run clear when a chicken thigh is pierced with a skewer.

Remove the chicken from the oven, cover with foil and leave to rest for 20 minutes. To serve, transfer the chicken to a platter, then scatter over a few coriander leaves and a little extra toasted shredded coconut. Pour over the pan juices and serve with lime cheeks for squeezing.

Note: this recipe can also be made keto-friendly in no time! Simply swap the coconut aminos for sugar-free fish sauce and you're all set.

Charcoal chicken schnitzel with lime and mayo ⑤

SERVES 4

These delicious schnitzels are a fantastic way of getting the health benefits of activated charcoal into your life, plus they look incredible on the plate. You will blow your friends and family away with this one!

4 x 180 g chicken thigh or breast fillets
85 g (½ cup) arrowroot or tapioca flour
4 eggs
125 ml (½ cup) coconut milk
200 g (2 cups) almond meal
1 tablespoon activated charcoal powder
2 teaspoons garlic powder
2 teaspoons onion powder
1 teaspoon chilli powder
1 teaspoon sweet paprika
sea salt
coconut oil, for deep-frying
freshly ground black pepper

To serve
lime wedges
150 g (½ cup) Mayo (see page 262)
Charred Veggie Salad (see page 96) (optional)

Place the chicken pieces between two sheets of baking paper. Using a rolling pin or mallet, bash the pieces into even, flat escalopes about 1–2 cm thick.

Put the arrowroot or tapioca flour in a shallow bowl. In a second bowl, whisk the eggs and coconut milk until thick and creamy. In a third bowl, mix the almond meal, charcoal powder, spices and 1 teaspoon of salt until the mixture turns black.

Now it's time to crumb! Working with one piece of chicken at a time, dip into the flour, then into the egg mixture and finally into the almond meal mixture to coat evenly, shaking off any excess coating as you go.

Half-fill a large heavy-based saucepan with coconut oil and set over medium heat. Heat the oil to 160°C. To test if it is hot enough, simply drop a small piece of bread into the oil – if it sizzles immediately, you're good to go.

Working in batches, carefully lower the schnitzels into the hot oil. Fry for 8–10 minutes, turning halfway through, until crispy and cooked through. Remove from the oil and drain on paper towel. Season generously with salt and pepper.

Divide the schnitzels among plates and serve with lime wedges and mayo, with my charred veggie salad on the side.

THE LOWDOWN

Get used to hearing more about activated charcoal now and in the years to come. For those who are not sure what it is, it's a potent natural detoxifying substance (usually in powder form). When ingested, it can help cleanse and flush our digestive system of toxins and poisons. Activated charcoal can be found in natural-health stores.

Adobo drumsticks with creamy cucumber salad

SERVES 2

Adobo is a very popular dish and cooking process in Filipino cuisine that involves marinating meat, seafood or vegetables in vinegar, soy sauce and garlic. I tried it while travelling and was blown away by how incredibly delicious it was, so I just had to share my healthy interpretation of this classic dish with you.

2 tablespoons coconut oil
4 large or 6 medium chicken drumsticks
2 garlic cloves, crushed
1 brown onion, roughly chopped
1 long red chilli, finely chopped
125 ml (½ cup) coconut aminos
1 tablespoon apple cider vinegar
1 teaspoon sugar-free fish sauce
zest and juice of 4 limes

Creamy cucumber salad
2 Lebanese cucumbers, halved lengthways, seeds removed, sliced
1 spring onion, finely sliced
2 large handfuls of coriander leaves, finely chopped
2 large handfuls of mint leaves, shredded
3 tablespoons coconut yoghurt or coconut cream
1 garlic clove, very finely chopped
juice and zest of 2 limes

Melt 1 tablespoon of the coconut oil in a large heavy-based saucepan over medium heat. Add the drumsticks and cook, turning, for 3–4 minutes, or until sealed and browned on all sides. Remove from the pan and set aside.

Melt the remaining tablespoon of coconut oil in the pan, add the garlic, onion and chilli and cook for 4–5 minutes, or until softened and caramelised.

Return the chicken to the pan, along with the coconut aminos, apple cider vinegar, fish sauce and lime zest and juice. Bring to a simmer, then reduce the heat to low and cook, covered, for 1 hour, or until the chicken is lovely and tender and the sauce is sticky and thick, stirring regularly to baste the drumsticks in the sauce.

While the drumsticks are cooking, make the cucumber salad. Combine the cucumber, spring onion, coriander and mint in a bowl. In a separate bowl, mix the coconut yoghurt or cream, garlic and lime zest and juice to make a creamy dressing.

When ready to serve, drizzle the coconut dressing over the cucumber salad and serve alongside the adobo drumsticks.

Note: you can make this recipe keto by simply adjusting the quantity of coconut aminos. Reduce the amount to 3 tablespoons and mix with 125 ml (½ cup) of water before adding to the rest of your ingredients.

Pistachio and lemon–crusted lamb backstraps (K)(LC)(S)

SERVES 4

Lamb is definitely one of my favourite meats thanks to its rich, full-on fatty flavour! But did you know that lamb can also offer you a trim, lean cut of protein? Trimmed from the middle of the loin, the lamb backstrap is a cut that comes from the back of the animal near the spine and is free from fat, gristle and bone – making it perfect for using with a flavoursome crust like this.

3 tablespoons extra-virgin olive
  oil or melted butter
4 x 200 g lamb backstraps
sea salt and freshly ground
  black pepper

Pistachio and lemon crust
2 garlic cloves, crushed
75 g (½ cup) roughly chopped
  pistachios
2 large handfuls of flat-leaf
  parsley leaves, finely chopped
2 large handfuls of mint leaves,
  finely chopped
zest of 1 lemon
1 teaspoon dijon mustard
½ teaspoon sea salt
¼ teaspoon freshly ground
  black pepper

To serve
green salad leaves
Coconut Cauliflower Puree
  (see page 143)

Preheat the oven to 180°C and line a baking tray with baking paper.

To make the crust, add all the ingredients to a bowl and stir well to combine.

Drizzle half the oil or butter over the backstraps and rub it into the meat to coat evenly. Heat a frying pan over high heat and add the lamb. Cook, turning, for 1–2 minutes on each side to seal the lamb. Remove from the pan and set aside until it is cool enough to touch. Using your hands, press the pistachio and lemon crust all over the surface of the meat, then drizzle over the remaining oil or butter. Season well with salt and pepper.

Carefully transfer the backstraps to the prepared baking tray and roast for 12–14 minutes, or until golden brown and medium–rare when cut into with a sharp knife. Set aside to rest for 5 minutes, then cut into thin slices and serve with a few green salad leaves and my coconut cauliflower puree.

THE LOWDOWN

When I recommend people celebrate nuts in their diet, they sometimes come back wondering if they might be eating the wrong types of fat. Well, I have good news for them and you alike: the fats found in nuts, including pistachios, work to improve your blood cholesterol levels and help combat cardiovascular disease, while also providing a great source of energy.

Bengal beef bites

MAKES 12

Based on a traditional Indian recipe, these Bengal beef bites sit somewhere on the scale between a fritter and a croquette. Give these amazing little morsels a go and I reckon you'll fall in love with them just as I have.

2 sweet potatoes (700–800 g), peeled and diced
80 ml (⅓ cup) coconut oil or butter
sea salt and freshly ground black pepper
250 g beef mince
2 tablespoons coconut flour
2 teaspoons dijon mustard
1 teaspoon onion powder
1 egg
65 g (½ cup) arrowroot or tapioca flour

To serve
2 Lebanese cucumbers, sliced
Smoky Mayo (see page 109)

Add the sweet potato to a large saucepan of boiling water and cook for 10–12 minutes, or until soft. Drain, then return the sweet potato to the pan over medium heat, along with 1 tablespoon of the oil or butter and roughly mash with a fork or potato masher. Cook, stirring, for 3–4 minutes to remove any excess moisture and to get rid of any big lumps, then transfer to a bowl and season well with salt and pepper. Set aside.

Melt another tablespoon of oil or butter in a frying pan over medium heat. Add the beef mince and cook, breaking it up with the back of a wooden spoon, until just browned (be careful not to overcook it). Transfer the mince to the bowl with the sweet potato. Add the coconut flour, dijon mustard, onion powder and egg, and mix everything together really well with your hands. Cover with plastic wrap and transfer to the fridge for 30 minutes to chill and firm.

Once firm, take 2 tablespoons of the mixture and shape it with your hands into a pyramid shape. Transfer to a baking tray or platter and repeat with the rest of the mixture to make 12 pyramids.

Place the arrowroot or tapioca flour in a bowl and coat each pyramid, making sure to cover all sides.

Heat the remaining oil or butter in a frying pan over medium–high heat. Working in manageable batches, add the beef bites and fry for 2–3 minutes on each side, or until crispy and nicely golden brown. Once cooked, remove from the pan and place on paper towel to absorb any excess oil.

Pile the bites onto a platter and serve with cucumber slices and some hot, smoky mayo for dipping. Enjoy!

Luscious lamb kofta Ⓚ ⓛⒸ Ⓢ Ⓝⓕ

SERVES 4

Usually served on sticks or skewers, we know kofta from Greek food, although they belong to the same family as the meatball and meatloaf dishes of South Asian, Middle Eastern, Balkan and Central Asian cuisines. I love them because they celebrate one of my favourite types of mince – lamb. Lamb mince is particularly flavoursome, due to its good-quality fat content. I hope you love them too!

800 g lamb mince
1 red onion, finely chopped
2 garlic cloves, very finely chopped
2 tablespoons finely chopped mint leaves
2 tablespoons finely chopped flat-leaf parsley
2 teaspoons sweet paprika
2 teaspoons ground cumin
2 teaspoons ground coriander
1 teaspoon cayenne pepper
1 teaspoon sea salt

To serve
2 large handfuls of mint leaves, finely chopped
Avocado Tzatziki (see page 120)

Place 12 bamboo skewers in a shallow dish, cover with cold water and leave to soak for at least 30 minutes.

Heat a barbecue grill or chargrill pan to medium–high.

In a large bowl, mix all the ingredients really well using your hands so that the flavourings are evenly distributed through the mince.

Scoop a small handful (about ⅓ cup) of the mixture out of the bowl and mould it into a sausage shape around 10 cm long around the end of one of the prepared skewers. Press down on the mix with your fingertips to bind the meat to the skewer, then transfer to the prepared baking tray and repeat with the remaining mixture and skewers.

Grill for 3–4 minutes on each side, or until the kofta are cooked through. They should be a lovely golden brown colour and only a little pink on the inside. Divide among serving plates, scatter over some chopped mint and serve with my avocado tzatziki.

TIP

These are also fantastic baked in the oven. Simply preheat the oven to 180°C and line a tray with baking paper. Place the kofta skewers on the tray and bake for 15–20 minutes.

Chicken karaage with ponzu dipping sauce (S) (NF)

SERVES 4

Karaage is a Japanese term for chicken that's coated in starch or flour and fried. Like gyoza and ramen, it's an example of a dish that has been adapted from the Chinese culinary culture and transformed into something uniquely Japanese. I was first introduced to it when a Japanese takeaway shop opened on the route I would walk home from school. The fried chicken they served was well worth saving my tuckshop money for – I hope you feel the same about these!

800 g chicken thigh fillets, halved lengthways
250 g (2 cups) arrowroot or tapioca flour
coconut oil, for deep-frying
sea salt and freshly ground black pepper

Marinade
125 ml (½ cup) coconut cream
5 cm piece of ginger, finely sliced
2 garlic cloves, finely sliced
3 spring onions, finely sliced
3 tablespoons coconut aminos
1 tablespoon coconut oil, melted

Paleo 'ponzu' dipping sauce
3 tablespoons coconut aminos
1 tablespoon very finely chopped ginger
1 garlic clove, very finely chopped
juice of 1 lemon

Wasabi mayo
300 g (1 cup) Mayo (see page 262)
1–2 teaspoons wasabi powder

To make the marinade, add all the ingredients to a large bowl and whisk well to combine. Add the chicken and toss until well coated, then transfer to the fridge and leave to marinate for at least 2 hours or overnight (if you really don't have any time you can set it aside in the fridge and carry on with the recipe; the flavour just won't be as full on).

Place the arrowroot or tapioca flour in a shallow bowl. Remove one of the chicken pieces from the marinade and roll it in the flour to cover completely, then shake off any excess flour and transfer to a plate or tray. Repeat with the remaining chicken.

For the ponzu dipping sauce, whisk the ingredients in a small bowl to combine. Set aside.

For the wasabi mayo, combine the ingredients in a small bowl. Set aside.

Half-fill a large heavy-based saucepan with coconut oil and set over medium heat. Heat the oil to 170°C. To test if it is hot enough, simply drop a small piece of bread into the oil – if it sizzles around the edges straight away, you're good to go.

Working in batches of two or three chicken pieces at a time, carefully lower the chicken into the hot oil and cook, turning halfway through, for 12 minutes, or until golden brown and crispy on all sides. Using metal tongs or a slotted spoon, remove from the pan and transfer to paper towel to drain off any excess oil. Repeat with the remaining chicken, then season with salt and pepper. Transfer to a serving platter and serve with the ponzu dipping sauce and wasabi mayo.

Easy cauliflower pizzas three ways

SERVES 4–6

I love pizza – I mean, who doesn't? The only problem is I can never decide which toppings I want! If you're like me, then don't worry, with these versatile mini pizzas I've got you sorted. Make multiples of your favourite, or go all out and make all three versions below. Either way, you are going to love these.

800 g (4 cups) Cauliflower Rice
  (see page 262)
100 g (1 cup) almond meal,
  plus extra if needed
2 tablespoons arrowroot or
  tapioca flour
2 eggs, beaten
2 teaspoons dried oregano
1 teaspoon sea salt
1 tablespoon extra-virgin olive oil

Roast chicken topping
1 teaspoon tomato paste
100 g shredded chicken (see
  page 173)
6 cherry tomatoes, quartered
basil leaves, to serve

Prawn topping
1 teaspoon tomato paste
100 g Chermoula Tiger Prawns,
  roughly chopped (see page 133)
1 tablespoon pesto
4 cherry tomatoes, quartered
juice of ¼ lemon
toasted pine nuts, to serve

Chargrilled vegetable topping
1 teaspoon tomato paste
100 g chargrilled zucchini,
  capsicum and eggplant
4 cherry tomatoes, quartered
baby rocket leaves, to serve

Preheat the oven to 180°C and line two large baking trays with baking paper.

Make the cauliflower rice as instructed, then leave to cool. Once it is cool enough to touch, pile it up in the centre of a dry tea towel, gather the ends together, twist and firmly squeeze out any excess water.

Add the cauliflower rice to a large bowl together with the almond meal, arrowroot or tapioca flour, egg, oregano and salt and stir well to combine. The mixture should be dough-like in consistency – if it's looking a little crumbly, simply add some more almond meal until it holds together.

Using a spoon, dollop your 'dough' onto the prepared baking trays and spread out into three 12–15 cm rounds, about 5 mm thick. Bake for about 30–40 minutes or until lightly golden.

Remove from the oven, add your chosen toppings and place back in the oven for 10 minutes, or until the edges of the bases are golden brown and the toppings are heated through. Remove from the oven and top with your chosen garnish ingredients, drizzle over the olive oil and serve.

Los pollos nachos ⓢ

SERVES 4-6

For fans of Breaking Bad *and* Better Call Saul *out there, you'll see I have named these chicken nachos after the fictional chicken takeaway shop featured in the shows. I couldn't help myself! Introducing los pollos nachos, something I'd love to see on their menu!*

2 tablespoons extra-virgin olive oil, coconut oil or butter
4 garlic cloves, finely chopped
1 brown onion, finely chopped
1 long red chilli, roughly chopped
1 teaspoon ground cumin,
1 teaspoon ground coriander
1 teaspoon smoked paprika
1 teaspoon dried oregano
6 chicken thigh fillets
1 tablespoon apple cider vinegar
250 ml (1 cup) chicken stock
1 x 400 g can chopped tomatoes
coriander leaves, to serve

Sweet potato chips
1 large sweet potato, very finely sliced using a mandoline
3 tablespoons coconut oil, melted
sea salt

Avocado cream
2 avocados
2 tablespoons coconut cream
2 teaspoons extra-virgin olive oil
zest and juice of 1 lime
sea salt and freshly ground black pepper

Tomato salsa
4 tomatoes, finely diced
½ red onion, finely diced
1 bunch of coriander leaves, roughly chopped
1 long red chilli, finely chopped
zest and juice of 1 lime
2 tablespoons extra-virgin olive oil
sea salt and freshly ground black pepper

Cashew cheese
150 g (1 cup) cashew nuts, soaked in water for 1 hour
125 ml (½ cup) filtered water
½ teaspoon sea salt
zest and juice of 1 lemon
pinch of freshly ground black pepper

Preheat the oven to 160°C.

Heat the oil or butter in a large, flameproof casserole dish over medium heat, add the garlic, onion and chilli and saute for 3–4 minutes, or until softened and caramelised. Stir in the spices and oregano, add the chicken thighs and saute for 3–4 minutes, or until the chicken is sealed and browned on all sides. Add the apple cider vinegar, chicken stock and chopped tomatoes and bring to a simmer. Remove from the heat, carefully transfer to the oven and cook, uncovered and turning the chicken pieces halfway through, for 45–50 minutes, or until the meat is tender and the liquid has mostly evaporated. Remove from the oven and set aside to cool slightly, then shred the chicken pieces with two forks.

For the sweet potato chips, line a baking tray with baking paper. Add the sweet potato slices to a bowl and drizzle all over with the coconut oil. Toss well to coat, then spread over the prepared baking tray in a single layer. Bake for 5 minutes, then flip and cook for a further 2 minutes, or until golden and crispy. (Be careful not to burn these beauties as they cook pretty fast!) Season with salt and set aside.

To make the avocado cream, whiz everything together in the bowl of a food processor until smooth. Cover with plastic wrap and keep in the fridge until needed.

For the tomato salsa, combine all the ingredients in a bowl. Season to taste with salt and pepper and set aside for the flavours to develop.

To make the cashew cheese, blitz all the ingredients in a food processor until smooth and creamy.

When ready to serve, pile the sweet potato chips into a serving bowl. Spoon over the shredded chicken, scatter over some coriander leaves and top with generous dollops of the avocado cream, salsa and cashew cheese.

The ultimate souvlaki (S)

SERVES 4

This is Greek fast food at its finest! The first souvlaki shops in Greece appeared in Livadia in 1951, selling souvlaki on a rotating skewer. Whether served on the skewer, plated with fried potatoes, or (my favourite) stuffed into pita sandwiches with garnishes and sauces, it's a truly awesome dish, and this version made with paleo pitas is one I simply can't get enough of.

3 tablespoons extra-virgin olive oil
2 garlic cloves, very finely chopped
zest and juice of 2 lemons
2 teaspoons dried oregano
sea salt and freshly ground
  black pepper
800 g chicken thigh fillets,
  roughly chopped
Avocado Tzatziki (see page 120),
  to serve (optional)

Greek salad
2 tomatoes, finely diced
1 Lebanese cucumber, finely
  diced
¼ red onion, finely diced
2 large handfuls of flat-leaf
  parsley leaves, finely chopped
1 tablespoon extra-virgin olive oil

Paleo pitas
100 g (1 cup) almond meal
125 g (1 cup) arrowroot or
  tapioca flour
125 ml (½ cup) coconut milk
125 ml (½ cup) filtered water
1 teaspoon dried oregano
pinch of sea salt
3–4 tablespoons coconut oil

Place eight bamboo skewers in a shallow dish, cover with cold water and leave to soak for at least 30 minutes.

Add the olive oil, garlic, lemon zest and juice and oregano to a large bowl and mix together well. Season with salt and pepper to taste, add the chicken and toss to coat, then cover with plastic wrap and set aside in the fridge to marinate for at least 20 minutes (or up to 3 hours if you've got time).

To make the Greek salad, toss together all the ingredients in a bowl.

For the pitas, combine the almond meal, arrowroot or tapioca flour, coconut milk, water, oregano and salt in a bowl and mix well to form a smooth batter. Melt about 1 tablespoon of the coconut oil in a small non-stick frying pan over medium heat. Ladle one-quarter of the batter into the pan, tilting and swirling it to coat the base in an even layer, and cook for 2–3 minutes, then carefully turn the pita over with a spatula and cook for a further 2 minutes, or until golden and cooked through. Repeat with the remaining mixture, greasing the pan with a little extra coconut oil in between pitas to make sure they don't stick to the pan. Set aside wrapped in a clean tea towel to keep warm.

Heat a barbecue grill or chargrill pan to medium–high.

Thread the marinated chicken onto the prepared skewers and grill for 6–8 minutes on each side, or until cooked through and nicely charred on the outside. Remove from the heat and leave to cool slightly.

To assemble the souvlaki, spoon a few generous dollops of avocado tzatziki (if using) on each pita. Top with a chicken skewer and a few spoonfuls of the salad. Wrap up and enjoy.

NYC cheeseburger bowl

SERVES 2

Whenever I go to the States, without fail I have to get my burger hit on the day I land – it just feels (and tastes) so right! For similar reasons I just had to include this simple recipe for an all-American cheeseburger bowl here – it is super easy to create, tastes great, and fulfils any of those cravings you might be having for takeaway, while actually being pretty great for you. So what are you waiting for? It's time to get stuck in to your first burger bowl!

400 g beef mince
1 teaspoon onion powder
1 teaspoon garlic powder
sea salt
1–2 tablespoons extra-virgin olive
  oil, coconut oil or butter
1 baby cos lettuce, leaves
  separated
1 large tomato, sliced
2–4 pickled gherkins, sliced
  lengthways
½ red onion, sliced
freshly ground black pepper
2 tablespoons dijon mustard

'Cheese'
2 tablespoons coconut oil
  or butter
1 yellow zucchini or 100 g
  summer squash, cut into cubes
1 carrot, finely diced
½ red onion, diced
1 garlic clove, finely chopped
½ teaspoon dijon mustard
½ teaspoon sea salt
250 ml (1 cup) coconut cream
1 egg yolk
sea salt and freshly ground
  black pepper

To make the 'cheese', melt the coconut oil or butter in a heavy-based saucepan over medium heat. Add the zucchini or squash, carrot, onion, garlic, mustard and ½ teaspoon of salt and saute for 5–10 minutes, or until the veggies have started to soften and the onion is translucent. Pour over the coconut cream, bring to a simmer and cook for 5 minutes, then cover with a lid and cook for a further 5 minutes, or until the veggies are nice and soft. Remove from the heat and set aside to cool slightly, then transfer to a food processor or blender and whiz until nice and smooth. Add the egg yolk and whiz again – the egg will thicken the sauce and give it a richer texture. Season to taste and set aside.

Add the mince, onion powder, garlic powder and salt to a bowl. Using your hands, mix everything really well so that the flavourings are evenly distributed through the mince, then divide into two even-sized chunky patties.

Heat the oil or butter in a frying pan over medium heat, add the patties and cook for 8 minutes, then flip and cook for a further 6–8 minutes, or until nicely golden on the outside (it's okay if they are still slightly pink in the middle as they will continue to cook through once they leave the pan).

Divide the burger patties between shallow bowls, arrange the lettuce leaves around the patties and top with the 'cheese', tomato, pickled gherkins and onion. Season to taste with salt and pepper and serve with the mustard on the side. Devour!

Kickin' fried chicken (LC) (S)

SERVES 4

Here you go guys! Follow Colonel Luke's recipe by rubbing your drumsticks in my not-so-secret blend of herbs and spices and I guarantee you'll soon be whipping up the tastiest fried chicken in your own kitchen. In fact, I reckon you'll be blown away by how this simple flavour combination takes these drumsticks to the next level. This is fried chicken done right!

extra-virgin olive oil or coconut
   oil, for cooking
250 ml (1 cup) coconut milk
2 eggs
100 g (1 cup) almond meal
65 g (½ cup) arrowroot or
   tapioca flour
1 teaspoon dried parsley
½ teaspoon dried sage
½ teaspoon dried basil
1 teaspoon sweet paprika
1 teaspoon chilli powder
½ teaspoon ground ginger
½ teaspoon mustard powder
¼ teaspoon Chinese five-spice
¼ teaspoon sea salt
8 chicken drumsticks, skin on

To serve
Smoky Mayo (see page 109)
Zesty Slaw (see page 92)

Preheat the oven to 180°C. Line a baking dish with baking paper and fill it with oil to a depth of 2–3 mm.

Whisk the coconut milk and eggs together in a shallow bowl. In another bowl, combine the almond meal, arrowroot or tapioca flour, dried herbs, spices and salt.

Coat one of the chicken drumsticks with the coconut milk and egg mixture, then shake off any excess liquid before dipping into the almond meal mixture to coat evenly. Place the coated drumstick in the prepared baking dish and repeat with the remaining drumsticks.

Transfer the baking dish to the oven and bake for 45 minutes, turning two or three times through cooking, until lovely and golden and super crispy on all sides. Serve with my smoky mayo and zesty slaw.

Sensational shepherd's pie

SERVES 4-6

While traditional shepherd's pie is topped with potato, which many of us following a lower-carb approach try to avoid, this low-carb version opts instead for a cauliflower puree. Slow-cooked, rich, yummy mince topped with creamy cauliflower – what's not to love?

1 tablespoon extra-virgin olive oil, coconut oil or butter
4 garlic cloves, finely chopped
2 celery stalks, finely diced
2 carrots, finely diced
1 brown onion, finely diced
1 teaspoon ground cumin
700 g lamb mince
3 tablespoons tomato paste
1 teaspoon roughly chopped thyme leaves
500 ml (2 cups) beef stock
½ bunch flat-leaf parsley leaves, roughly chopped
salad leaves, to serve

Cauliflower topping
800 g cauliflower, broken into florets, stalk roughly chopped
2 tablespoons extra-virgin olive oil, coconut oil or butter
sea salt and freshly ground black pepper

Preheat the oven to 180°C.

Heat the oil or butter in a large frying pan over medium–high heat. Add the garlic, celery, carrot, onion and cumin and saute for 4–5 minutes, or until the onion starts to soften and caramelise.

Increase the heat to high, add the mince and cook, stirring, for 6–8 minutes or until browned all over. Stir in the tomato paste and thyme and cook for a further 1–2 minutes, then pour over the stock. Reduce the heat to medium and simmer, stirring occasionally, for 10–15 minutes, or until the sauce has thickened slightly and the flavours have melded together.

Meanwhile, make the cauliflower topping. Add the cauliflower to a saucepan of boiling water and cook for 8–10 minutes, until tender. Drain, then transfer to a food processor and blitz until smooth. Add the oil or butter and pulse to combine, then season generously to taste.

To assemble the shepherd's pie, spoon the mince mixture into an ovenproof dish in an even layer, then top with the cauliflower puree and smooth the surface with the back of a spoon or spatula.

Bake for 30–40 minutes, or until the cauliflower topping is lightly golden. Remove from the oven, scatter over the chopped parsley and serve with your favourite salad leaves.

Curried chicken pie

SERVES 4

Curried pies are super famous in the UK and, if I have anything to do with it, they'll soon be just as popular here. After all, what could be more delicious than a creamy chicken curry topped with crispy pastry? And when that pastry is made out of low-carb, gluten- and dairy-free ingredients, well now, that's pretty much as good as it gets!

2 tablespoons extra-virgin olive oil, coconut oil or butter, plus extra to brush
2 garlic cloves, very finely chopped
1 brown onion, roughly chopped
1 celery stalk, finely chopped
1 carrot, roughly chopped
1 long red chilli, finely chopped
360 g mushrooms, roughly chopped
525 g leftover shredded roast chicken
125 ml (½ cup) coconut cream
1 tablespoon arrowroot or tapioca flour
2 teaspoons curry powder
1 teaspoon ground turmeric
130 g baby spinach leaves
sea salt and freshly ground black pepper
green salad leaves, to serve

Pastry
50 g (½ cup) almond meal
60 g (½ cup) coconut flour
40 g (⅓ cup) arrowroot or tapioca flour
½ teaspoon sea salt
125 g butter, chilled and cut into 3 cm cubes
1 egg
3 tablespoons cold filtered water
½ teaspoon apple cider vinegar

To make the pastry, combine the almond meal, coconut flour, arrowroot or tapioca flour and salt in a bowl. Add the butter and rub it in with your fingertips until the mixture resembles fine breadcrumbs. Add the egg, water and apple cider vinegar and mix together with your hands to form a nice, sticky paste-like dough. Roll into a ball, cover with plastic wrap and transfer to the fridge to rest for 20 minutes.

Meanwhile, heat the oil or butter in a large frying pan over medium heat. Add the garlic, onion, celery, carrot and chilli and saute for 5–6 minutes, or until the veggies have softened and are starting to caramelise.

Add the mushroom to the pan and cook for 4–5 minutes, or until reduced, then add the chicken and coconut cream and cook, stirring, for 1–2 minutes. Add the arrowroot or tapioca flour, curry powder and turmeric and cook, stirring for 2–3 minutes, then stir in the spinach leaves and cook for another 1–2 minutes, or until the leaves are wilted and the sauce is thick and creamy. Season with salt and pepper to taste, remove the pan from the heat and spoon the mixture evenly into four 10 cm wide ramekins.

Preheat the oven to 180°C.

Remove the pastry from the fridge and roll it out between two sheets of baking paper to 3 mm thick. Remove the top sheet of baking paper and, using a 10 cm round cutter, cut into four equal-sized rounds.

Place one of the pastry circles on top of a ramekin, crimp the edges with a fork to seal, then brush with a little oil or butter. Repeat with the remaining pastry circles and ramekins.

Arrange the pies on a baking tray, transfer to the oven and bake for 20–30 minutes, or until the pastry is golden. Serve up the individual pies with crisp, green salad leaves.

TIP

You can also make this recipe in one large pie dish if you wish (a 20 cm round dish should do the job). And don't waste any leftover pastry – use it to decorate the tops of your pies in whatever patterns you like.

Singapore noodles (LC) (S) (NF)

SERVES 4

Breaking news guys – despite its name, this delicious dish was not created in Singapore (where it is also rarely eaten), but is instead very commonly found in Cantonese-style restaurants and takeaway eateries in Hong Kong. There's a fun fact to share with your friends, and here's a pretty awesome healthy version of the dish to share while you're at it.

4 zucchini
3 tablespoons coconut oil
2 eggs, beaten
4 chicken thigh fillets, sliced
2 garlic cloves, chopped
2 long red chillies, finely chopped
2 shallots, finely sliced
1 red capsicum, deseeded and finely sliced
5 cm piece of ginger, finely grated
300 g broccolini, roughly chopped
400 g raw king prawns, shelled and deveined
1 tablespoon sugar-free fish sauce
2 tablespoons coconut aminos
2 tablespoons curry powder
90 g (1 cup) bean sprouts, trimmed
sea salt and freshly ground black pepper
1 spring onion, finely sliced
1 handful of coriander leaves
lime cheeks, to serve

Using a mandoline, spiraliser or a sharp knife, cut the zucchini into fine vegetable noodles. Set aside.

Melt 1 tablespoon of the coconut oil in a large frying pan or wok over medium heat. Pour in the egg and tilt the pan to cover the base completely, then cook for 2–3 minutes without stirring, or until the omelette has set. Fold in half with a spatula, remove from the pan and slice into thin strips.

Heat the remaining coconut oil in the same pan, add the chicken, garlic, chilli, shallot, capsicum and ginger and stir-fry for 3–4 minutes, or until the vegetables have started to soften. Add the broccolini and stir-fry for a further 3–4 minutes, then add the prawns and cook for 1–2 minutes, or until they begin to change colour. Stir in the fish sauce, coconut aminos and curry powder and cook for a further 1–2 minutes, or until the prawns are cooked through.

Return the omelette slices to the pan along with the bean sprouts and zucchini noodles. Season with salt and pepper and cook, tossing occasionally, for 2 minutes, or until everything is heated through and well combined.

To serve, pile the Singapore noodles onto a large platter or divide among individual shallow bowls. Scatter over the sliced spring onion and coriander leaves and serve with lime cheeks for squeezing.

Chicken korma curry

SERVES 4

'Korma' is the name given to a mild curry of meat or fish that is marinated in yoghurt or curds. This version swaps the yoghurt for coconut cream to provide you with a delicious dairy-free take on the original. It's a great curry to introduce kids to as it isn't super hot but allows their tastebuds to explore different levels of spice.

2 tablespoons extra-virgin olive oil, coconut oil or butter
1 large shallot, finely sliced
800 g chicken thigh fillets, cut into bite-sized chunks
1 x 400 ml can coconut cream
500 g butternut pumpkin, peeled and cut into bite-sized chunks
sea salt and freshly ground black pepper

Korma curry paste
4 garlic cloves
2 tablespoons tomato paste
2 shallots
4 cm piece of ginger, peeled
1 bunch of coriander
1 tablespoon ground cumin
1 tablespoon ground coriander
2 teaspoons garam masala
1 teaspoon sea salt
1 teaspoon cayenne pepper
1 tablespoon extra-virgin olive oil or coconut oil

To serve
800 g (4 cups) Cauliflower Rice (see page 262)
2 large handfuls of coriander leaves
2 tablespoons fried shallots (optional)

To make the korma curry paste, blitz all the ingredients in a food processor until smooth. Measure out 125 g (½ cup) of the paste and set the remainder aside for another use (see tip).

Heat the oil or butter in a large saucepan over medium heat, add the shallot and 125 g (½ cup) curry paste and saute for 2–3 minutes, or until really lovely and fragrant. Make sure you keep stirring as you go so the paste doesn't stick to the bottom of the pan and burn.

Increase the heat to high, add the chicken and saute for 4–5 minutes, or until brown on all sides. Stir in the coconut cream and bring to the boil, then reduce the heat to medium, add the pumpkin and simmer, covered with a lid but stirring occasionally, for 10–15 minutes, or until the pumpkin is beautiful and tender.

Spoon the curry into bowls, season with salt and pepper and serve alongside cauliflower rice sprinkled with coriander and fried shallots (if using). Yum!

TIP

Leftover korma curry paste will keep in an airtight container in the fridge for up to 7 days or in the freezer for up to 3 months.

Chicken tikka tandoori

SERVES 4

Tandoori chicken is a famous Indian dish of roasted chicken marinated in yoghurt and spices. This version offers up a dairy-free alternative to the classic, though still including all the flavours you know and love.

1 x 1.5 kg whole chicken, cut into quarters (ask your butcher to do this for you)

Tandoori marinade
1 tablespoon coriander seeds
1 tablespoon cumin seeds
1 teaspoon fennel seeds
4 cardamom pods, seeds only
5 whole cloves
8 garlic cloves, peeled
5 cm piece of ginger, roughly chopped
zest and juice of 2 limes
3 tablespoons coconut cream
2 tablespoons extra-virgin olive oil or coconut oil
1 teaspoon sea salt
1 teaspoon sweet paprika
1 teaspoon cayenne powder

Green chutney
1 small brown onion
1 handful of mint leaves
1 handful of coriander leaves
1 bird's eye chilli
juice of 1 lemon
½ teaspoon sea salt
½ teaspoon coconut sugar

To make the marinade, add the coriander, cumin, fennel and cardamom seeds and cloves to a spice grinder or the small bowl of a food processor and blitz to form a powder. Transfer to a blender or large bowl of a food processor, add the remaining ingredients and whiz until smooth. Pour the mixture over the chicken pieces and turn them to coat all over, then cover the bowl with plastic wrap, transfer to the fridge and leave to marinate for 15–20 minutes, or even 3 hours to overnight if you want to prepare it in advance.

For the green chutney, add all the ingredients to a food processor and pulse together until well combined.

Preheat the oven to 200°C and line a baking tray with baking paper.

Remove the marinated chicken from the fridge and arrange on the prepared baking tray. Bake in the oven for 20–25 minutes, turning halfway through cooking, until golden brown and cooked through. Pile onto a platter and drizzle over the green chutney.

TIP

Leftover chutney can be stored in an airtight container in the fridge for up to 1 week.

Red-hot rendang (LC) (S) (NF)

SERVES 4

Originating in Indonesia, a traditional rendang is hot, spicy and full of flavour, and is something I really enjoy eating when travelling in South-East Asia. This version delivers all the above and is a great way of getting the fantastic flavours of traditional Indonesian food into your home with an abundance of healthy ingredients to boot!

2 tablespoons coconut oil
1 x 1–1.5 kg beef brisket, trimmed and quartered
sea salt
2 x 400 ml cans coconut cream
750 ml (3 cups) beef stock
2 tablespoons sugar-free fish sauce
6 kaffir lime leaves
1 lemongrass stalk, white part only, bruised
3 tablespoons lime juice

Rendang curry paste
2 tablespoons coriander seeds
½ teaspoon white peppercorns
40 g (½ cup) desiccated coconut, toasted
4 long red chillies, roughly chopped
2 shallots, roughly chopped
4 garlic cloves, roughly chopped
5 cm piece of galangal, peeled, roughly chopped
5 cm piece of ginger, roughly chopped
2 cm piece of fresh turmeric, peeled, roughly chopped
1 lemongrass stalk, white part only, finely sliced
4 kaffir lime leaves, shredded
1 tablespoon coconut sugar
2 tablespoons coconut oil

Coconut sambal
110 g (2 cups) coconut flakes
2 tablespoons sugar-free fish sauce
zest and juice of 1 lime
1 tablespoon coconut sugar
1 bunch of coriander leaves
1 red or green chilli, roughly chopped

Preheat the oven to 180°C.

Heat the oil in a large ovenproof heavy-based saucepan, frying pan or flameproof casserole dish over high heat.

Season the beef well with salt, then add to the pan and saute for 3–4 minutes, or until sealed and browned on all sides. Transfer to a plate and set aside.

To make the curry paste, toast the coriander seeds and peppercorns in a small dry frying pan over medium heat for 2–3 minutes, or until aromatic, then transfer to a food processor and blitz to a powder. Add the remaining paste ingredients and blitz until smooth.

Set your ovenproof pan or dish back over medium heat, add the curry paste and cook, stirring, for 1–2 minutes, or until fragrant. Pour over the coconut cream, stock and fish sauce, add the kaffir lime leaves, lemongrass stalk and sealed beef brisket and bring to the boil. Cover the pan or dish with a lid, transfer to the oven and cook for 4 hours, turning the brisket over after 2 hours of cooking, until the beef is lovely and tender and the sauce has thickened and reduced and is beautifully aromatic.

While the rendang is cooking, make the coconut sambal. Add all the ingredients to a food processor and blitz together to form a rough, chunky paste. Set aside.

When ready to serve, remove the rendang from the oven, drain away any excess oil and stir through the lime juice. Divide among plates and top with dollops of the coconut sambal.

Hot and spicy chicken nuggets

SERVES 4

Don't be fooled into thinking that just because these are called nuggets they are for the little ones – I've created this recipe with adults in mind, adding some serious heat to give this childhood favourite a boost. Who said you can't order from the children's menu?

700 g chicken thigh fillets,
  cut into bite-sized chunks
125 g (1 cup) arrowroot or
  tapioca flour
45 g (½ cup) desiccated coconut
55 g (½ cup) almond meal
½ teaspoon sea salt
coconut oil, for deep-frying
lime zest, to serve (optional)
150 g (½ cup) Smoky Mayo
  (see page 109)

Spicy marinade
2 long red chillies, finely diced
2 large garlic cloves, very finely
  chopped
2 tablespoons coconut aminos
1 teaspoon chilli powder
1 teaspoon smoked paprika
1 teaspoon sea salt
zest and juice of 1 lime

To make the spicy marinade, place all the ingredients in a large bowl and mix well to combine. Add the chicken and toss until well coated, then transfer to the fridge and leave to marinate for at least 20 minutes (or up to 2 hours if you've got time).

In a large zip-lock bag or bowl, mix together the arrowroot or tapioca flour, desiccated coconut, almond meal and salt. Shake off any excess marinade from the chicken pieces, then add to the bag or bowl and either seal and shake or mix together to ensure the meat is coated all over.

Half-fill a large heavy-based saucepan with coconut oil and set over medium heat. Heat the oil to 160°C. To test if it is hot enough, simply drop a small piece of bread into the oil – if it sizzles around the edges straight away, you're good to go.

Working in batches, carefully lower the chicken into the hot oil and fry, turning halfway through, for 4–5 minutes, or until golden brown and crisp all over. Using metal tongs or a slotted spoon, remove the chicken from the pan and transfer to paper towel to drain. Transfer to a serving platter, scatter over some lime zest (if desired) and serve with my smoky mayo for dipping.

Luke's lovely lasagne

SERVES 4

When I was little, I loved my mum's awesome lasagne. Here I've taken my favourite elements and given them the Luke Hines twist to present you my lovely lasagne. Whisper it, but I think it's even better than the original – sorry Mum!

1 large eggplant, sliced into
   1 cm thick discs
sea salt and freshly ground
   black pepper
80 ml (⅓ cup) extra-virgin olive
   oil, coconut oil or butter, plus
   extra for greasing
2 parsnips, cut into 1 cm
   thick discs
2 large handfuls of basil
   leaves, torn
10 button mushrooms, sliced
90 g (2 cups) baby spinach leaves
4 zucchini, sliced lengthways into
   thin ribbons

Rich tomato ragu
2 tablespoons extra-virgin olive
   oil, coconut oil or butter
1 brown onion, finely diced
2 garlic cloves, very finely
   chopped
2 celery stalks, finely diced
600 g beef mince
3 tablespoons tomato paste
1 teaspoon sweet paprika
1 teaspoon chilli powder
750 ml (3 cups) tomato passata
250 ml (1 cup) beef stock
sea salt and freshly ground
   black pepper

Cauliflower 'cheese' sauce
1 head of cauliflower, cut into
   small florets
500 ml (2 cups) coconut cream
3 tablespoons arrowroot or
   tapioca flour
1 egg, beaten

Season the eggplant slices generously with salt, transfer to a colander in the sink and set aside for 10 minutes to draw out any excess water. Rinse and pat dry.

Melt 1 tablespoon of the oil or butter in a large frying pan over high heat, add the eggplant in small batches and cook for 2–3 minutes on each side, or until soft and caramelised around the edges. Transfer to a plate, then repeat with the remaining slices, adding an extra tablespoon or so of oil or butter to the pan between batches if needed. Set aside.

To make the ragu, heat the oil or butter in a large saucepan over medium heat. Add the onion, garlic and celery and saute for 3–4 minutes, or until the veggies have softened and are starting to caramelise. Increase the heat to high, add the mince and brown off evenly, breaking it up with a wooden spoon. Stir in the tomato paste, paprika and chilli powder and cook, stirring, for a further 3–4 minutes, then pour over the passata and stock and season generously with salt and pepper. Bring to the boil, then reduce the heat to a simmer and cook, uncovered, for 10–15 minutes, or until the sauce has thickened and reduced. Remove from the heat and set aside.

Preheat the oven to 180°C and grease a 35 x 25 cm baking dish with oil or butter. Cover the base of the dish with the parsnip discs in an even overlapping layer, drizzle over the remaining oil or butter and bake for 10–12 minutes, until the parsnip is soft and lightly golden.

Remove the dish from the oven and spoon half the ragu over the parsnip, then layer over the eggplant and scatter over the basil leaves and mushroom. Spoon over the rest of the ragu and top with the baby spinach leaves and zucchini ribbons, then gently press everything down with your fingertips to firm the lasagne up. Bake for 30 minutes.

Meanwhile, steam the cauliflower for 10–15 minutes, or until tender. Whisk the coconut cream and arrowroot or tapioca flour in a saucepan over medium heat to combine, then bring to the boil, reduce the heat to a simmer and cook, stirring, for 10–15 minutes until thickened. Remove from the heat and stir in the egg and cauliflower, then transfer the mixture to a food processor and blitz to a smooth, creamy sauce.

Pour the cauliflower 'cheese' sauce over the lasagne and cook for a further 15 minutes, until golden brown on top. Enjoy!

Phenomenal pulled pork

SERVES 8-10

Pulled pork exploded onto the foodie scene a couple of years back when dude food took off, and it has never looked back. Unlike many food trends that come and go, pulled pork is here to stay and for good reason – it's nutritious, incredibly delicious and very easy to prepare at home (though you will need to start this recipe the day before eating).

1 x 2 kg pork shoulder, bone in
250 ml (1 cup) chicken, beef
  or pork stock
125 ml (½ cup) apple cider
  vinegar
125 ml (½ cup) coconut aminos
1 x 400 g can crushed tomatoes
2 dried bay leaves
shredded kaffir lime leaves,
  to garnish (optional)
Cabbage Slaw (see page 138)
  or Zesty Slaw (see page 92),
  to serve

Rub
1 tablespoon smoked paprika
2 teaspoons dried chilli flakes
2 teaspoons ground coriander
2 teaspoons ground cumin
2 teaspoons freshly ground
  black pepper
1 teaspoon ground cinnamon
2 garlic cloves, crushed
1 tablespoon sea salt

For the rub, combine all the ingredients in a bowl.

Place the pork shoulder in a large dish, tip the rub over the top and use your fingers to press it all over the meat, taking care to get it into all the folds and fatty bits. Cover with plastic wrap, transfer to the fridge and leave overnight to allow the rub to penetrate the surface of the meat and get as much yummy flavour into it as possible.

The next day, preheat the oven to 180°C.

Combine the stock, apple cider vinegar, coconut aminos, crushed tomatoes and bay leaves in a large baking dish, then lay over the pork shoulder and cover loosely with foil. Roast for 4–6 hours, turning and basting the pork with the sauce every hour, until the meat is so tender it falls apart when pressed with a fork.

Remove the dish from the oven and shred the meat using two forks. Discard the bone, stir the shredded meat into the sauce and cook for a further 20 minutes, or until the sauce has thickened up nicely. Divide the pulled pork among plates, scatter over some shredded kaffir lime leaves (if using) and serve with your choice of slaw.

Slow-cooked Turkish lamb with eggplant smash (K) (LC) (S) (NF)

SERVES 4-6

I absolutely love this Turkish-inspired take on slow-cooked lamb shoulder. If you have time, you can try marinating the lamb in the yoghurt and spices for a few hours (or overnight) before you start cooking to add even more depth of flavour, though I must say it tastes pretty fantastic without this. The silky eggplant smash makes the perfect accompaniment – I just know this is going to be a massive crowd pleaser in your house.

3 tablespoons cumin seeds
1 tablespoon dried chilli flakes
2 tablespoons sea salt
1 tablespoon freshly ground
  black pepper
250 ml (1 cup) coconut cream
80 ml (⅓ cup) extra-virgin olive
  oil, plus extra for drizzling
1 x 1–1.5 kg lamb shoulder,
  bone in
flat-leaf parsley leaves, to serve

Eggplant smash
2 large eggplants, peeled, cut
  lengthways into 1 cm thick slices
sea salt
2 tablespoons extra-virgin olive oil
2 garlic cloves
2 tablespoons coconut yoghurt or
  coconut cream
1 tablespoon tahini
1 teaspoon ground cumin
zest and juice of 1 lemon

Preheat the oven to 180°C and line a baking tray with baking paper.

Lightly toast the cumin seeds in a small dry frying pan until fragrant, then transfer to a bowl together with the chilli flakes, salt and pepper and mix together well. In a separate bowl, whisk together the coconut cream and olive oil.

Using your fingers, rub the lamb really well with the coconut cream and oil mixture, then sprinkle over the spice mix to coat as evenly as possible. Transfer the lamb shoulder to a roasting tin, cover loosely with foil and bake for 2–3 hours, or until the meat is so tender it falls apart when pressed with a fork. Remove from the oven and leave to rest, covered with foil, for 30 minutes.

Meanwhile, make the eggplant smash. Season the eggplant slices generously with salt, transfer to a colander in the sink and set aside for 10 minutes to draw out any excess water. Rinse and pat dry, then arrange the eggplant slices on the prepared baking tray, drizzle with 1 tablespoon of the olive oil and bake for 30 minutes, or until very soft.

Transfer the eggplant to a food processor together with the remaining 1 tablespoon of oil and the rest of the smash ingredients, and blitz until lovely and smooth.

When ready to serve, transfer the lamb shoulder to a large serving platter. Scatter over some parsley leaves, drizzle over a little olive oil and serve alongside the eggplant smash.

Smoky wings Ⓚ Ⓛⓒ Ⓢ Ⓝⓕ

SERVES 4

Cheap, nutritious and flavoursome, chicken wings are one cut of meat you really should look at getting into your diet! They can be jazzed up with all sorts of flavour combinations, but this smoky paprika spice rub is up there as one of my all-time favourites – it's a fantastic way of getting loads of flavour into the wings without having to wait around for ages for them to marinate.

2 tablespoons smoked paprika
1 tablespoon dried chilli flakes
1 tablespoon sea salt
2 teaspoons coconut sugar
2 teaspoons ground sumac
2 teaspoons freshly ground
  black pepper
600 g chicken wings
2 tablespoons extra-virgin
  olive oil
lime halves, to serve

Preheat the oven to 180°C and line a baking tray with baking paper.

Add the paprika, chilli flakes, salt, coconut sugar, sumac and black pepper to a bowl and mix well. In a separate large bowl, toss the chicken wings with the olive oil until well coated.

Tip the spice rub over the wings, reserving a pinch or two for sprinkling, and massage it into the meat with your hands, making sure they are well coated.

Place the wings on the prepared baking tray in a single layer and bake for 20–30 minutes, turning halfway through cooking, until golden and cooked through.

Pile the wings onto a serving platter, sprinkle over the reserved rub and serve with lime halves for squeezing.

TIP

While I like to add all of this smoky rub to these wings as I like things nice and spicy, you might prefer your wings a bit milder, so feel free to hold a bit back for your next cook-up.

The perfect crispy pork belly with broccolini, apple and mint salad (LC) (S) (NF)

SERVES 4–6

If there is one thing that I have learned over my years of cooking it is that perfectly cooked, crispy pork belly is the ultimate crowd pleaser. And I have good news for you – getting crispy crackling every time is easier than you might think! Follow my trusty technique below for the best crackle of your life.

1 x 1 kg piece of pork belly, skin on, scored
630 g (2 cups) coarse rock salt, plus extra if needed

Marinade
125 ml (½ cup) filtered water
125 ml (½ cup) coconut aminos
2 garlic cloves, very finely chopped
1 tablespoon honey or pure maple syrup
1 tablespoon ground coriander
1 tablespoon ground cumin

Broccolini, apple and mint salad
10 broccolini florets, stems removed
125 ml (½ cup) extra-virgin olive oil
sea salt
3 tablespoons coconut milk
2 garlic cloves, finely grated
2 tablespoons tahini
juice of 2 lemons
1 teaspoon dried chilli flakes
1 bunch mint, leaves picked
4 granny smith apples, cored and thinly sliced into discs

Preheat the oven to 180°C and line a roasting tin with baking paper.

To make the marinade, mix all the ingredients in a bowl. Pour the marinade into the prepared roasting tin, then place the pork belly, flesh-side down, on top. Using paper towel, pat the skin dry. If your belly is not sitting evenly in the tin, use some rolled-up foil to level it out so the skin is level and flat. Fill the pan with water to about 2 cm below the pork skin, then carefully pour the salt over the skin, spreading it all the way to the edges, to form a thick layer. (You want to be sure the skin is not visible, so add a little extra salt if necessary – it will turn into a solid crust during cooking.)

Carefully transfer the tin to the oven, being careful not to wet the pork skin, and roast for 40 minutes. Remove from the oven and carefully lift the solid salt crust off the skin, using a pastry brush to remove any stray granules. Increase the oven temperature to 240°C, return the pork to the oven and cook for a further 30–40 minutes, or until the skin has puffed up and crisped to a lovely crackling. You can also place the pork under a hot grill for a few minutes to crisp up the skin even further if necessary.

While the pork is cooking, make the broccolini, apple and mint salad. Heat a barbecue grill or chargrill pan to medium–high. Coat the broccolini with one-quarter of the olive oil and season well with salt, then transfer to the barbecue or chargrill pan and cook for 4–5 minutes, or until charred and tender. Set aside.

Combine the remaining olive oil, coconut milk, garlic, tahini, lemon juice and chilli flakes in a bowl and whisk to make a dressing.

Remove the cooked pork belly from the oven and transfer to a board or tray, then use a cleaver or large sharp knife to cut it into chunks. Arrange the broccolini, mint and apple slices in a serving bowl, drizzle over the dressing and toss to coat. Serve alongside the pork belly.

Balinese beef short ribs

SERVES 4–6

I love Bali, not just for the sun and surf (of which I am obviously a massive fan) but also for the incredible food – Indonesian cuisine has an incredible way of packing so much flavour and vibrancy into dishes using such simple ingredients. These short ribs take inspiration from that, transporting those same super-exciting flavours to your home kitchen.

1.5 kg beef short ribs, cut into
    4–6 pieces (ask your butcher
    to do this for you)
500 ml (2 cups) filtered water
sea salt and freshly ground
    black pepper

Spice paste
4 lemongrass stalks, white parts
    only, bruised
4 garlic cloves, very finely
    chopped
2 cm piece of ginger, finely
    chopped
1 brown onion, finely diced
3 tablespoons coconut aminos
2 tablespoons sugar-free
    fish sauce
zest and juice of 1 orange
zest and juice of 1 lime
1 teaspoon dried chilli flakes
½ teaspoon Chinese five-spice
pinch of salt

To serve
Cauliflower Rice (see page 262) or
    Broccoli Rice (see tip)
coriander leaves
toasted peanuts
lime cheeks

Preheat the oven to 200°C.

To make the spice paste, blitz the lemongrass, garlic, ginger and onion in a food processor until well combined. Add the remaining ingredients and blitz again until combined.

Place the ribs in a large roasting tin and pour over the prepared spice paste. Using your hands, rub the mixture into the meat to coat evenly, then pour the water into the tin and cover tightly with foil.

Roast for 30 minutes, then remove the tin from the oven. Very carefully peel the foil back and turn the ribs over. Re-cover with foil, return to the oven and cook for a further 30 minutes before reducing the oven temperature to 170°C and cooking for another 2 hours, turning halfway through. To finish the ribs off, remove the foil, crank the heat back up to 200°C and cook, uncovered, for 15–20 minutes, or until the ribs are lovely and caramelised.

Serve the ribs on a bed of cauliflower or broccoli rice, scattered with coriander leaves and toasted peanuts, along with a few lime cheeks for squeezing.

TIP

Broccoli rice is the delicious green cousin of cauliflower rice. Follow the same method (see page 262) simply using broccoli florets instead of cauliflower.

Middle Eastern meatballs with za'atar (K) (LC) (S) (NF)

SERVES 4

If there is one thing I love doing, it's exploring the cuisines of other countries in my kitchen by playing with different combinations of fresh herbs and spices. In this super-easy recipe I've done exactly that, using za'atar – a Middle Eastern spice blend made with sesame seeds, thyme and sumac – to deliver a delicious flavour to these moreish meatballs.

500 g beef mince
2 tablespoons extra-virgin olive oil, coconut oil or butter, plus extra for cooking
1 brown onion, finely chopped
1 garlic clove, very finely chopped
2 tablespoons very finely chopped flat-leaf parsley leaves
2 tablespoons very finely chopped mint leaves
1 teaspoon sea salt
1 teaspoon ground cumin
½ teaspoon freshly ground black pepper

Za'atar
1 tablespoon sesame seeds
3 tablespoons ground sumac
2 tablespoons dried thyme
2 tablespoons dried marjoram
2 tablespoons dried oregano
1 teaspoon sea salt

To serve
baby gem lettuce leaves
coconut yoghurt

To make the za'atar, toast the sesame seeds in a dry frying pan over medium heat for 4–5 minutes, stirring regularly, until golden and aromatic. Transfer to a food processor or mortar and pestle and briefly pulse or crush to a rough powder, then add the remaining ingredients and mix well.

To make the meatballs, place all the ingredients and 2 teaspoons of za'atar in a large bowl. Using your hands, mix everything together really well so that the flavourings are evenly distributed through the mince. Roll small handfuls of the mince into walnut-sized balls and flatten them slightly with the palm of your hand.

Heat a barbecue grill or chargrill pan to medium–high and brush with oil or butter. Add the meatballs and cook for 2 minutes on each side, or until nicely charred on the outside but still a little pink in the centre.

Serve the meatballs wrapped in lettuce leaves with some coconut yoghurt for dipping.

TIP

Leftover za'atar will keep in an airtight container in a cool, dark place for 3–6 months. It's perfect for sprinkling over smashed avocado on toast or chargrilled vegetables.

Chargrilled pork skewers

SERVES 4

Although I love to eat it, for a long time I was put off cooking pork as I always tended to overcook it. Thankfully, I've learned different ways to cook it – such as these chargrilled skewers – that ensure it remains moist, tender and bursting with flavour. I just can't get enough!

800 g boneless pork neck or pork
   fillets, cut into 2 cm thick strips
sea salt and freshly ground
   black pepper
1 bird's eye chilli, finely chopped
3 tablespoons peanuts, toasted
1 handful of edible flowers or
   micro herbs (such as coriander,
   mint or parsley)
honey or pure maple syrup,
   to serve (optional)
lime cheeks, to serve

Marinade
125 ml (½ cup) coconut milk
125 ml (½ cup) tahini
2 tablespoons sugar-free
   fish sauce
1 tablespoon honey or pure
   maple syrup
juice of 2 limes

Place eight bamboo skewers in a shallow dish, cover with cold water and leave to soak for at least 30 minutes.

To make the marinade, combine all the ingredients in a bowl. Transfer half the mixture to a separate large bowl, add the pork and toss until well coated, then set aside for 10 minutes to marinate.

Heat a barbecue grill or chargrill pan to medium.

Thread the marinated pork onto the prepared skewers and season with well with salt and pepper. Grill the skewers, basting with the remaining marinade as you go, for about 3 minutes on each side, or until cooked through and nicely charred on the outside.

Transfer the cooked skewers to a serving platter. Scatter over the chilli, toasted peanuts and edible flowers or micro herbs and drizzle over a little more honey or maple syrup if you like a little extra sweetness. Serve with lime cheeks for squeezing over.

Luke's lamb ribs

SERVES 4

Lamb ribs are a fantastic, nutritious and affordable meal for the whole family. I especially love to prepare them like this as it takes less time than many other rib recipes, while still being super simple and delivering truckloads of really delicious, complex flavours.

1–1.5 kg lamb rib racks, trimmed
  of any excess fat
mint leaves, to serve

Spice paste
3 tablespoons apple cider vinegar
2 tablespoons granulated
  coconut sugar
1½ tablespoons extra-virgin
  olive oil
2 tablespoons ground cumin
2 tablespoons ground coriander
2 tablespoons dried chilli flakes
½ tablespoon sea salt
1 teaspoon freshly ground
  black pepper

Apple cider relish
125 ml (½ cup) apple cider
  vinegar
2 tablespoons coconut sugar
1 garlic clove, very finely chopped
2 large handfuls of mint leaves,
  roughly chopped

Preheat the oven to 160°C and line a baking tray with baking paper.

For the spice paste, mix together all the ingredients in a bowl.

Using your fingers, generously rub the rib racks with the spice paste and then place, skin-side up, on the prepared baking tray. Cover with foil and seal around the edges, then transfer to the oven and bake for 2 hours. Remove the foil, increase the temperature to 220°C and cook for a further 10 minutes, or until the ribs are caramelised and golden brown.

While the ribs are cooking, make the apple cider relish. Add the apple cider vinegar, sugar and garlic to a saucepan over high heat, bring to a simmer and cook for 2–3 minutes, or until slightly syrupy. Remove from the heat and set aside to cool slightly, then stir through the chopped mint.

Remove the rib racks from the oven, cover with foil and leave to rest for 10 minutes.

To serve, slice up the rib racks and pile them on a serving platter. Scatter over some mint leaves and devour with the relish.

TREATS & DESSERTS

Coconut ice

MAKES 10 PIECES

When I was growing up, coconut ice was one of my all-time favourite treats as I loved both the flavour and the amazing pink colour of the top layer! I think I have always been attracted to treats that aren't too sweet and feel really substantial to eat, and my version of coconut ice is certainly one of those – it will definitely hit the spot without delivering any of the original's processed and refined sugars.

540 g (6 cups) desiccated coconut
500 g coconut butter, softened
250 ml (1 cup) coconut cream
1 vanilla pod, split and seeds
  scraped, or 1 teaspoon vanilla
  powder
1 tablespoon fresh beetroot juice
½ teaspoon stevia

Line a 23 cm square cake tin with baking paper.

Place the desiccated coconut, coconut butter, coconut cream and vanilla in a food processor and pulse until really well combined and smooth.

Pour half the mixture into the prepared cake tin and flatten the surface with a spoon or palette knife so it is nice and even all over. Transfer to the fridge or freezer and leave for 15–20 minutes, or until set firm.

Add the beetroot juice and stevia to the remaining ingredients in the food processor. Pulse together until smooth, really well combined and a beautiful pink colour. Pour the mixture over the set white layer, flattening it out into an even layer, and return the tin to the fridge or freezer to set until firm, about 15–20 minutes.

To serve, remove the coconut ice from the cake tin and cut into squares. Any leftovers can be stored in an airtight container in the fridge for up to 7 days.

TIP

Fresh beetroot juice can be found in most health-food stores and some supermarkets, but if you are struggling to get your hands on any, you can always whip some up by running some fresh peeled beetroot through a powerful juicer.

THE LOWDOWN

The fantastic thing about coconut is that it boosts your metabolism, encouraging the energy in the foods you consume to be burned as fuel rather than stored as body fat. Plus it is high in lauric acid, which can boost your immune system and protect against viral and bacterial infections.

Choc-nut fudge (K) (LC) (S) (V)

MAKES 15 PIECES

When I am winding down after a big day I often start to crave chocolate – I absolutely love the stuff! Being mindful of staying on track with my health and fitness goals though, I steer clear of the processed or refined sugars found in the conventional stuff and instead turn to homemade chocolate (see page 224) as well as this super delicious chocolate peanut fudge – it's the perfect low-carb healthy alternative to have to hand.

125 ml (½ cup) coconut oil
125 ml (½ cup) coconut cream
60 g (½ cup) cacao powder
250 g peanut butter, smooth
 or crunchy
1 vanilla pod, split and seeds
 scraped, or 1 teaspoon vanilla
 powder
½ teaspoon stevia or to taste
dried rose petals, to serve
 (optional)

Line a 20 cm square cake tin with baking paper.

Melt the coconut oil in a saucepan set over medium heat, add the coconut cream and cacao powder and stir to combine. Stir in the peanut butter, vanilla and stevia and cook, stirring, for 3–4 minutes, or until the peanut butter is completely incorporated into the mixture.

Pour the mixture into the prepared cake tin, transfer to the fridge and leave for at least 30 minutes, or until set.

To serve, cut into chunky pieces and sprinkle over some dried rose petals if you like. Any leftovers can be stored in an airtight container in the fridge for up to 7 days or in the freezer for up to 3 months.

TIP

Not a fan of peanut butter or simply following a strict paleo approach and wanting to avoid peanuts? That's fine – all other nut butters work really well here too. And if you have a nut allergy that's also not a problem – just swap the nut butter for the same quantity of tahini for a fantastic nut-free alternative!

Coconut cookie dough bites

MAKES 30 BITES

Cookie dough is certainly celebrated more in American culture, but once you've tried it, you'll be hard pressed to disagree with why it's so popular! This recipe takes a typical raw cookie dough and substitutes the usual nasties for good-fat, low-carb ingredients, to deliver a taste sensation that won't disappoint.

250 g macadamia nut butter
90 g (1 cup) desiccated coconut
80 g (½ cup) macadamia nuts,
  roughly chopped
1 tablespoon cacao nibs
¼ teaspoon stevia
1 vanilla pod, split and seeds
  scraped, or 1 teaspoon vanilla
  powder
½ teaspoon ground cinnamon
pinch of salt

Line a baking tray with baking paper.

Add all the ingredients to a food processor and pulse until they come together. Roll a tablespoonful of the mixture into a ball, then transfer to the prepared baking tray. Repeat with the rest of the mixture, then transfer to the fridge and leave for 20 minutes for the dough bites to chill and firm.

TIPS

These balls can be popped into an airtight container and kept in the freezer to be enjoyed later for up to 3 months.

Got some of my homemade chocolate (see page 224) to hand? Try melting it down and drizzling it over these bad boys!

Chocolate bars 4 ways

MAKES ABOUT 600 G OF CHOCOLATE

I think you are going to absolutely love this recipe for making your own rich, nutritious dark chocolate, which tastes great as it is and is pretty amazing when given any of my favourite four flavour enhancements. Cacao is a natural mood elevator and anti-depressant – so get your happy on with this easy and delicious recipe!

Luke's dark chocolate
220 g (1 cup) cacao butter, melted
120 g (1 cup) cacao powder
250 g macadamia nut or
  peanut butter
½ teaspoon stevia
1 vanilla pod, split and seeds
  scraped, or 1 teaspoon vanilla
  powder

The hot pink (S only)
3 tablespoons honey or pure
  maple syrup
¼ teaspoon hot chilli powder
generous pinch of pink salt

The raspberry bomb
  (LC & S only)
125 g (1 cup) fresh or frozen
  raspberries

The 'Bounty'
3 tablespoons coconut cream
3 tablespoons flaked or
  shredded coconut

The fruit 'n' nut
70 g (½ cup) hazelnuts, toasted,
  roughly chopped
30 g (¼ cup) dried unsweetened
  blueberries

To make the dark chocolate, combine all the ingredients in a food processor and blend for 2–3 minutes, or until smooth and silky. (Alternatively, melt the cacao butter together with the remaining ingredients in a saucepan over medium–low heat, stirring regularly, until lovely and runny.)

Either keep plain or add your preferred flavourings as per the options below, then pour into a chocolate mould, cupcake patties or a very small baking tray lined with baking paper. Sprinkle over your chosen ingredients, if using, then transfer to the fridge and leave for 30 minutes, or until set firm. Store in a suitable airtight container in the fridge for up to 1 month, or in the freezer for up 3 months.

For the hot pink, replace the stevia in the dark chocolate recipe with the honey or maple syrup. Add the chilli powder to the melted chocolate mixture and sprinkle with pink salt flakes before setting.

For the raspberry bomb, add half the raspberries to the melted chocolate mixture and scatter the bar with the remainder before setting.

For the 'Bounty', swirl the coconut cream through the melted chocolate mixture and sprinkle the bar with the shredded coconut before setting.

For the fruit 'n' nut, stir the hazelnuts and blueberries into the melted chocolate mixture before setting.

TIP

Cacao butter is the fat derived from the cacao bean. It looks very much like white chocolate and can be found in most health-food stores in chunks, slabs, bars or buttons.

THE LOWDOWN

Cacao is packed full of health benefits – it is the highest plant-based source of iron, contains 40 times more antioxidants than blueberries and more calcium than cow's milk. It is also packed with magnesium, which is essential for healthy heart and brain function.

Chocolate crackles

MAKES 6 LARGE OR 12 REGULAR-SIZED CRACKLES

Looking for a bite-sized, keto-friendly treat to get you through your day feeling energised, while curbing cravings and managing blood-sugar levels? Well, look no further than these chocolate crackles.

110 g (½ cup) cacao butter
60 g (½ cup) cacao powder
30 g (½ cup) flaked coconut
50 g (½ cup) pecans, crushed
2 tablespoons coconut oil,
   plus extra to grease
2 tablespoons coconut cream
1 vanilla pod, split and seeds
   scraped, or 1 teaspoon vanilla
   powder
¼ teaspoon stevia
pinch of salt

Grease a large 6-hole or regular 12-hole muffin tin with coconut oil and line with paper cases.

Melt the cacao butter with the cacao powder in a saucepan over medium–low heat, stirring, until smooth and creamy. Stir in the remaining ingredients to combine, then spoon the mixture evenly into the paper cases and place in the fridge for about 30 minutes to set.

Enjoy straight away, or keep in an airtight container in the fridge for up to 1 week or in the freezer for up to 3 months.

THE LOWDOWN

They say you are what you eat and in the case of pecans – which look like mini brains – they are pretty much right! Pecans contain copper, which is necessary for healthy brain function, as well as manganese, which is known to help alleviate mood problems and focusing issues.

Salted almond butter cups

MAKES 6

You guys know I love a good nut butter cup! For this book I wanted to see if I could create a keto/paleo version suitable for all of those out there following this low-carb, high-fat, grain- and legume-free lifestyle! It can be done, and here is how!

125 ml (½ cup) coconut cream, water reserved (see tip)
125 ml (½ cup) coconut oil
60 g (½ cup) cacao powder
⅛ teaspoon stevia
1 vanilla pod, split and seeds scraped, or 1 teaspoon vanilla powder
2 tablespoons cacao nibs

Almond butter layer
125 g almond butter
2 tablespoons coconut oil
½ teaspoon ground cinnamon
⅛ teaspoon stevia
generous pinch of pink salt

Line a 6-hole muffin tin with paper cases.

Warm the coconut cream and coconut oil in a saucepan over medium–low heat, stirring to combine, until lovely and runny. Add the cacao powder, stevia and vanilla and whisk gently until well combined, then remove from the heat.

Pour half the melted chocolate mixture evenly into the paper cases, then transfer to the freezer and leave to set.

Meanwhile, make the almond butter layer. Place all the ingredients in a small saucepan over low heat and stir until the almond butter has melted and the mixture is nice and smooth.

Once your chocolate layer is set, spoon evenly sized dollops of the almond butter mixture over the chocolate bases until all the mixture is used. Return to the freezer to set.

To finish, pour the remaining chocolate over the set almond butter layer, sprinkle with the cacao nibs and return to the freezer until set. Enjoy straight away or transfer to an airtight container and keep in the fridge for up to 2 weeks or in the freezer for up to 6 months.

TIP

You can use the reserved coconut water in smoothies, curries, sauces and soups.

The ultimate one-pan cookie ⓢ

SERVES 6-8

How would you feel if I told you that you could make a giant cookie in a pan? Well, hold onto your socks boys and girls … things are about to get real. Introducing the ultimate one-pan cookie. You can thank me later.

200 g butter, chopped
125 ml (½ cup) honey or pure
  maple syrup
200 g (2 cups) almond meal
1 teaspoon gluten-free baking
  powder
1 teaspoon vanilla powder
½ teaspoon ground cinnamon
1 egg, beaten
3 tablespoons crunchy
  peanut butter
100 g Luke's Dark Chocolate (see
  page 224), roughly chopped
Whipped Vanilla Coconut Cream
  (see page 262) or coconut
  yoghurt, to serve

Preheat the oven to 180°C.

Melt the butter and honey or maple syrup in an ovenproof frying pan. Remove from the heat and leave to cool slightly, then stir in the almond meal, baking powder, vanilla and cinnamon. Whisk in the egg to form a batter.

Dollop the peanut butter over the batter and scatter over the chocolate pieces, then transfer the pan to the oven and bake for 20–25 minutes, or until golden brown and crispy on the outside.

Serve warm in the middle of the table for everyone to share, topped with a generous dollop of coconut cream or coconut yoghurt.

Purple doughnuts ⓢ

MAKES 12

Ube powder is a purple starch made in the Philippines from the purple yam. Its vibrant colour isn't the only thing I love – the yam is known to improve blood-sugar regulation and has also been shown to have significant antibacterial and antifungal properties. I reckon that makes these doughnuts pretty special!

200 g (1 cup) ube powder
300 ml coconut milk
1 vanilla pod, split and seeds scraped, or 1 teaspoon vanilla powder
165 ml pure maple syrup
7 eggs, separated
125 ml (½ cup) melted coconut oil or MCT oil, plus extra to grease
200 g (2 cups) almond meal
2 tablespoons gluten-free baking powder
1 teaspoon sea salt
1 teaspoon cream of tartar
125 g (1 cup) Luke's Dark Chocolate (see page 224), melted
2 tablespoons roughly chopped toasted hazelnuts, to serve

Topping
250 g (1 cup) vanilla coconut yoghurt
250 ml (1 cup) melted Luke's Dark Chocolate (see page 224)

Preheat the oven to 180°C. Line a baking tray with baking paper and grease a 12-hole doughnut tin or two 6-hole muffin tins with coconut oil.

In a food processor, combine the ube powder, coconut milk and vanilla and whiz together until really smooth. Add 125 ml (½ cup) of the maple syrup, the egg yolks and coconut oil and pulse a few times until incorporated, then add the almond meal, baking powder and salt and whiz again to form a lovely batter.

In a separate bowl, beat the egg whites and cream of tartar with an electric whisk until soft peaks form. Slowly pour in the remaining maple syrup, still beating, until stiff peaks form.

Gently fold the egg white mixture into the batter, then pour evenly into the prepared holes and bake for 20–25 minutes, or until golden brown and fluffy. Remove from the oven and leave to cool slightly, then transfer to a wire rack to cool completely.

Once your purple doughnuts have cooled, top with lashings of coconut yoghurt and drizzle over the melted chocolate to finish. These are sure to impress!

TIP

Ube powder is gradually becoming more widely available, and can be found in good Asian grocery stores and online health-food stores.

THE LOWDOWN

MCT oil is made up of medium-chain triglycerides, a special type of saturated fatty acid. It is believed to help boost your energy and improve cognitive function. MCT oil can be found at health-food stores or online.

Raw choc–mint slice

MAKES 8-10

The mint slice used to be one of my mum's favourite biscuits and I have fond memories of her treating herself to one with a cuppa after a long day of looking after us kids. And with four of us terrors to keep her hands full, it's no wonder she needed that many cups of tea and mint slice biscuits! Here is my healthy take on the famous biscuit we all know and love. Enjoy, Mum.

200 g (2 cups) pecans
80 ml (⅓ cup) honey or pure
   maple syrup
80 ml (⅓ cup) coconut oil
120 g (1 cup) cacao powder
½ teaspoon sea salt

Filling
465 g (3 cups) cashew nuts,
   soaked in water for at least
   2 hours, drained
125 ml (½ cup) coconut cream
125 ml (½ cup) coconut oil,
   melted
45 g (½ cup) desiccated coconut
3 tablespoons honey or pure
   maple syrup
5–10 drops food-grade
   peppermint essential oil
1 large handful of mint leaves

Topping
125 ml (½ cup) coconut oil or
   cacao butter, melted
60 g (½ cup) cacao powder
2 tablespoons pure maple syrup

Line a 30 x 20 cm cake tin with baking paper.

For the base, pulse all the ingredients in a food processor to a crumb-like consistency. Using your fingers, press the mixture evenly into the prepared cake tin, then transfer to the freezer and leave for 20 minutes to firm up.

For the filling, place all the ingredients in the food processor or a high-speed blender and blend until nice and creamy. Taste and add more peppermint oil if desired.

Remove the tin from the freezer and spread the peppermint filling evenly over the base, then return to the freezer for 1 hour to set.

For the topping, stir the ingredients in a saucepan over very low heat until smooth and chocolatey.

Remove the tin from the freezer again, pour over the chocolate mixture and spread evenly using the back of a spoon or a spatula. Return the tin to the freezer until completely set, about 30 minutes. To serve, cut into pieces with a warm knife.

Apple and blueberry coconut crumble

SERVES 4-6

I don't think many things beat a warm fruit crumble on a cold night, especially when topped with rich coconut cream. This recipe is a fantastic lower-carb version of the well-known winter warmer. Bake yourself a batch, rug up on the couch and imagine you're sitting by the fire in a snow chalet!

8 granny smith apples, peeled, cored and sliced
100 g butter, chilled and cut into small cubes
100 g (1 cup) almond meal
60 g (1 cup) shredded coconut
60 g (½ cup) pumpkin seeds
½ teaspoon stevia
200 g fresh or frozen blueberries
Whipped Vanilla Coconut Cream (see page 262) or coconut yoghurt, to serve

Preheat the oven to 180°C.

Place the apple slices and 1 tablespoon of water in a saucepan over medium heat and cook for 4–5 minutes, or until softened. Layer the apple over the base of a small baking dish or pie dish.

Mix together the butter, almond meal, shredded coconut, pumpkin seeds and stevia in a bowl with your fingertips until the mixture resembles coarse breadcrumbs.

Dot the blueberries evenly over the par-cooked apples and spread the crumble mixture over the top.

Bake for 20–30 minutes, or until the crumble topping is golden brown. Serve warm with whipped coconut cream or coconut yoghurt.

THE LOWDOWN

Green granny smith apples have a lower fructose content than their red counterparts, making them a fantastic option for those following a lower-carb approach. Plus they're high in fibre, which helps to keep the digestive tract clean and healthy.

Raw beetroot mud cakes with zesty lemon frosting (S) (V) (R)

MAKES 12

It's not often you get mud cakes that don't require any baking! I love this recipe because it's a great way to get nutrient-rich ingredients into your diet with ease, plus, I just so happen to think this frosting is one of the nicest things since sliced paleo bread!

400 g beetroot (about 2 medium beetroot), peeled and grated
160 g (1 cup) macadamia nuts
155 g (1 cup) cashew nuts
120 g (1 cup) cacao powder
3 tablespoons honey or pure maple syrup
3 tablespoons coconut flour
3 tablespoons coconut oil
2 tablespoons chia seeds
1 vanilla pod, split and seeds scraped, or 1 teaspoon vanilla powder
finely chopped macadamia nuts, to garnish

Lemon frosting
155 g (1 cup) cashew nuts
125 g (½ cup) coconut butter, softened
110 g (½ cup) cacao butter, melted
3 tablespoons honey or pure maple syrup
2 tablespoons macadamia nut butter
zest and juice of 2 lemons

Line a 12-hole muffin tin with paper cases.

Add all the ingredients to a food processor and blitz until really smooth, about 2–5 minutes depending on the strength of your processor. Spoon the mixture evenly into the paper cases, transfer to the freezer and leave for 1 hour to set.

Meanwhile, make the lemon frosting by blitzing together all the ingredients in the food processor until smooth and creamy. Transfer to a bowl.

Once the mud cakes are set, remove from the freezer, slather over the lemon frosting and sprinkle with some chopped macadamia nuts. Enjoy straight away or transfer to an airtight container and keep in the fridge for up to 7 days or in the freezer for up to 3 months.

Note: If you have any whipped coconut cream leftover from another recipe, use this for the frosting.

Low-carb carrot cakes

MAKES 12

We are all too familiar with the way food fads come and go. In the last few years, kale, dude food, pulled pork, matcha green tea and even turmeric have had their turn in the limelight, and each year something is just waiting to become the new 'in' thing! Well, guess what? Back in the day, carrot cake was named as one of the top five food fads of the 1970s. Who said fads don't last?

5 eggs
200 g butter, melted
½ teaspoon stevia
1 vanilla pod, split and seeds scraped, or 1 teaspoon vanilla powder
300 g carrots (about 5 medium carrots), grated
60 g (½ cup) chopped walnuts, plus extra crushed, toasted walnuts to serve (optional)
45 g (½ cup) desiccated coconut
155 g (1½ cups) almond meal
1 teaspoon ground cinnamon
1 teaspoon mixed spice
2 teaspoons gluten-free baking powder

Frosting
125 g butter
125 g cashew nut butter
125 ml (½ cup) coconut oil
125 ml (½ cup) coconut cream
2 tablespoons honey or pure maple syrup
1 vanilla pod, split and seeds scraped, or 1 teaspoon vanilla powder
zest and juice of 1 lemon

Preheat the oven to 180°C and line a 12-hole muffin tin with paper cases.

Beat the eggs, melted butter, stevia, and vanilla in a large bowl until well combined. Add the remaining ingredients and mix well to form a thick batter.

Spoon the batter evenly into the paper cases and bake for 40–45 minutes, or until a toothpick inserted into the centre of a muffin comes out clean. Set aside to cool.

To make the frosting, put everything in a food processor and blend until smooth and creamy. Transfer the mixture to a piping bag or zip-lock bag and place in the fridge to firm up slightly.

Once cool, cover the muffins generously with the frosting and finish with a sprinkling of crushed, toasted walnuts, if you like. Enjoy straight away or transfer to an airtight container and keep in the fridge for up to 7 days or in the freezer for up to 3 months.

Pumpkin spice cheesecake ⑤

SERVES 12

I used to live on Acland Street in St Kilda, which is famed, among other things, for its amazing cake shops – and living so close to all that deliciousness was certainly very tempting! If you're familiar with similar cheesecake temptation, then this delicious pumpkin cheesecake recipe has got you covered.

240 g (1½ cups) macadamia nuts
50 g (½ cup) pecans
3 tablespoons coconut oil or butter, melted
3 tablespoons honey or pure maple syrup
½ teaspoon ground cinnamon
½ teaspoon ground ginger

Filling
1 kg pumpkin, peeled and cut into 2.5 cm cubes
390 g (2½ cups) cashew nuts, soaked in water for at least 30 minutes, drained
125 ml (½ cup) coconut oil, melted
125 ml (½ cup) honey or pure maple syrup
3 tablespoons coconut sugar
zest and juice of 1 lemon
1 vanilla pod, split and seeds scraped, or 1 teaspoon vanilla powder
1 teaspoon ground cinnamon
½ teaspoon ground ginger
½ teaspoon ground nutmeg

To serve
Whipped Vanilla Coconut Cream (see page 262)
ground cinnamon
edible flowers

Preheat the oven to 180°C and line the bottom of a 20 cm springform cake tin with baking paper.

Place the macadamias and pecans in a food processor or high-speed blender and blitz for 1 minute to form a fine powder. Add the oil or butter, honey or maple syrup and spices and continue to blend until everything comes together to form a nice crust.

Using your hands, press the nut mixture into the bottom of the prepared cake tin. Bake for 15 minutes, or until golden brown. Remove from the oven and leave to cool.

To make the filling, add the pumpkin pieces to a large saucepan of boiling water and cook for 15–20 minutes, or until very tender when pressed with a fork. Drain and leave to cool, then transfer to a food processor or high-speed blender and blend to a puree. Add the remaining filling ingredients and blend on high for 2–3 minutes, or until smooth and creamy, scraping down the sides from time to time for even blending.

Pour the pumpkin filling over the cooled base and smooth the surface. Place in the freezer for 1–2 hours, or until set. Cover with plastic wrap and store in the fridge until ready to serve.

To serve, dollop or pipe the whipped vanilla coconut cream around the edge of the cake, sprinkle with a little cinnamon and scatter over some edible flowers.

'Iced VoVos' (LC) (S)

MAKES 14

When I was a kid, I loved an Iced VoVo biscuit and I wasn't alone – topped with pink fondant, a strip of jammy raspberry and a sprinkling of coconut, it's been an Aussie family favourite since 1906. This recipe is my healthy ode to the original, delivering those same lovely flavours but using nutrient-rich ingredients.

200 g (2 cups) almond meal
125 ml (½ cup) coconut oil or
   butter, melted
1 egg
¼ teaspoon stevia
1 vanilla pod, split and seeds
   scraped, or 1 teaspoon vanilla
   powder
desiccated coconut, for sprinkling

Pink icing
250 g (1 cup) coconut butter
125 ml (½ cup) coconut cream
1–2 teaspoons beetroot juice
   (fresh baby beets work
   well, too)
2 teaspoons honey or pure
   maple syrup

Raspberry chia jam
60 g (½ cup) fresh or frozen
   raspberries
1 tablespoon honey or pure
   maple syrup
1 tablespoon chia seeds

Preheat the oven to 180°C and line a baking tray with baking paper.

For the base, mix the almond meal, oil or butter, egg, stevia and vanilla in a bowl until you have a lovely dough. Roll into a ball and rest in the fridge for 10–15 minutes.

Remove the dough from the fridge and roll between two sheets of baking paper, until 1 cm thick. Using a knife or rectangular cookie cutter, cut the dough into 14 rectangular biscuits and carefully place on the prepared baking tray. Transfer to the oven and bake for 8–10 minutes, or until cooked through and lightly golden.

For the pink icing, mix the ingredients in a bowl or food processor until well combined. Transfer to a piping bag or zip-lock bag and place in the fridge to firm up slightly.

For the raspberry chia jam, place all the ingredients and 1 tablespoon of water in a blender and blitz until smooth. You may need to add some extra water to help it combine. Pour the mixture into a saucepan over medium heat and stir until it begins to bubble. Reduce the heat and whisk constantly for 3–5 minutes, or until thickened. Remove from the heat and place in the fridge to cool until ready to use.

To assemble, pipe two long strips of pink icing along the long edges of each biscuit, then fill the gap in the centre with a strip of raspberry chia jam. Sprinkle with desiccated coconut and enjoy.

The 'Picnic' bar Ⓢ

MAKES 12 BARS

For those who may not know, the Picnic is a lumpy-shaped chocolate bar consisting of milk chocolate, peanuts, chewy nougat, caramel, biscuits and puffed rice. In the 1970s the Australian slogan for Picnic was 'more like a banquet than a picnic' and that's exactly what my nutrient-dense version is – a banquet of deliciousness. Enjoy, legends!

125 ml (½ cup) coconut oil
150 g (1 cup) coconut sugar
120 g (1 cup) cacao powder
55 g (½ cup) almond meal
1 vanilla pod, split and seeds scraped, or 1 teaspoon vanilla powder
2 large eggs, beaten
¼ teaspoon sea salt

Caramel layer
250 g cashew or macadamia nut butter
125 ml (½ cup) honey or pure maple syrup
125 ml (½ cup) coconut oil
1 vanilla pod, split and seeds scraped, or 1 teaspoon vanilla powder
¼ teaspoon sea salt

Peanut layer
250 ml (1 cup) melted coconut oil or cacao butter
120 g (1 cup) cacao powder
3 tablespoons pure maple syrup
160 g (1 cup) peanuts, toasted
20 g (1 cup) puffed buckwheat, toasted (optional)

Preheat the oven to 180°C and line a 24 cm square cake tin with baking paper.

Add the coconut oil, coconut sugar and cacao powder to a saucepan over medium heat and whisk for 4–5 minutes, or until well combined and the sugar has dissolved. Stir in the almond meal, vanilla, egg and salt to form a batter, then remove from the heat, pour into the prepared cake tin and spread evenly. Bake for 10–15 minutes, or until a toothpick inserted into the centre comes out clean. Set aside to cool completely.

To make the caramel layer, add all the ingredients to a saucepan over medium–high heat and melt, stirring constantly, until nice and runny. Pour the caramel over the cooled brownie layer and transfer to the fridge for 30 minutes to set firm.

For the crispy peanut layer, add the coconut oil or cacao butter, cacao powder and maple syrup to a saucepan over medium heat and stir until nice and smooth. Stir in the toasted peanuts and buckwheat, if using, then pour over the cooled caramel layer and return to the fridge for another 30 minutes, or until set.

To serve, remove from the fridge and cut into bars with a warm knife. Store in an airtight container in the fridge for up to 5 days.

The ultimate keto cake

SERVES 10–12

This keto-friendly ice-cream cake is nutrient-dense and packed with flavour – perfect for those looking to keep their carbs super low without skimping on taste and treats. The recipe was inspired by some amazing little desserts I found in an LA health-food store that were just begging to be turned into a delicious cake like this!

500 ml (2 cups) coconut milk
180 g (2 cups) desiccated coconut
125 ml (½ cup) coconut oil,
  plus extra to grease
60 g (½ cup) cacao powder,
  plus extra to garnish
½ teaspoon ground cinnamon
1 vanilla pod, split and seeds
  scraped, or 1 teaspoon
  vanilla powder
pinch of sea salt
60 g (½ cup) fresh raspberries

Base
320 g (2 cups) macadamia nuts
120 g (1 cup) cacao powder
60 g (½ cup) shredded coconut
3 tablespoons coconut oil
¼ teaspoon stevia
1 vanilla pod, split and seeds
  scraped, or 1 teaspoon vanilla
  powder
pinch of sea salt

Line the base of a 23 cm springform cake tin with baking paper and grease with coconut oil.

For the base, add all the ingredients to a food processor and blitz to form a smooth paste. Using your fingers, press the mixture firmly and evenly into the bottom of the prepared cake tin, then transfer to the freezer for 20 minutes to chill and firm up.

While the base is chilling, add the coconut milk, desiccated coconut, coconut oil, cacao powder, ground cinnamon, vanilla and salt to the food processor and blitz until very smooth, about 4–5 minutes.

Remove the tin from the freezer, pour the coconut mixture over the base and spread evenly. Transfer to the fridge and leave for 2–3 hours to chill and set.

When ready to serve, scatter over the raspberries and dust with extra cacao powder. Cut into slices with a warm knife and enjoy!

Banana split brownies ⓢ

MAKES 10

These brownies celebrate all of the delicious flavours found in a chocolate banana split – taste a mouthful, close your eyes and you'll think you're eating the real thing! This is going to be a favourite with the kids, for sure.

125 g coconut oil or butter, softened
3 tablespoons peanut or almond nut butter
3 tablespoons honey or pure maple syrup
3 tablespoons coconut cream
4 eggs
200 g (2 cups) almond meal
120 g (1 cup) cacao powder
1 vanilla pod, split and seeds scraped, or 1 teaspoon vanilla powder
1 teaspoon gluten-free baking powder
60 g (½ cup) walnuts, roughly chopped
125 g (1 cup) Luke's Dark Chocolate (see page 224), broken into small pieces
pinch of salt

Banana frosting

1 banana
90 g coconut butter
65 g (½ cup) Luke's Dark Chocolate (see page 224), melted
125 g butter or coconut oil, softened
3 tablespoons peanut or almond nut butter

To serve

1 banana, sliced
2 tablespoons roughly chopped walnuts
125 ml (½ cup) Whipped Vanilla Coconut Cream (see page 262)
65 g (½ cup) Luke's Dark Chocolate (see page 224), melted

Preheat the oven to 180°C and line a 20 cm square brownie tin with baking paper.

Add the oil or butter, nut butter, honey or maple syrup and coconut cream to a bowl and whisk until well combined. Once incorporated, add the eggs and whisk again. Stir in the almond meal, cacao powder, vanilla and baking powder to form a batter, then gently fold through the walnuts and chocolate, trying to keep them as intact as possible.

Pour the batter into the prepared brownie tin and bake for 12–20 minutes, or until a skewer inserted into the centre comes out clean. Remove from the oven and set aside to cool completely.

To make the banana frosting, add all the ingredients to a food processor and blitz until smooth.

Slather the banana frosting over the cooled brownie and cut into 10 pieces. Serve topped with banana slices, chopped walnuts and dollops of whipped coconut cream, drizzling over a little melted chocolate to finish.

Wicked 'Wagon Wheels'

MAKES 6 LARGE OR 12 SMALL

What do you get when you combine fluffy marshmallow and tart raspberry jam between two delicious cookies and cover the lot with melted chocolate? The classic Wagon Wheel, of course! This super-healthy version is guaranteed to keep your tastebuds happy.

100 g walnuts, pecans or macadamia nuts
3 tablespoons honey or pure maple syrup
1 vanilla pod, split and seeds scraped, or 1 teaspoon vanilla powder
2 tablespoons coconut oil or butter, melted, plus extra if needed
pinch of sea salt

Jam
125 g (1 cup) fresh or frozen raspberries
1 tablespoon chia seeds

Marshmallow
155 g (1 cup) cashew nuts, soaked in water overnight, drained and rinsed
90 g (1 cup) desiccated coconut
125 ml (½ cup) coconut cream, plus extra if needed
3 tablespoons pure maple syrup or coconut nectar
pinch of sea salt

Chocolate coating
350 g Luke's Dark Chocolate (see page 224)

For the jam, whiz the raspberries and chia seeds in a food processor until smooth. Pour into a jar and chill in the fridge.

To make the biscuits, place all the ingredients in a food processor and blitz to form a sticky dough, adding a little more butter or coconut oil if you need it to help bring everything together. Roll the dough out between two sheets of baking paper to a 5 mm thickness, then cut out an even number of biscuits with a round cookie cutter of your preferred size. Arrange on a baking tray and transfer to the freezer for 20–30 minutes to firm.

While the biscuits are firming, make the marshmallow. Add all the ingredients to the food processor and blend until thick and creamy, adding a little extra coconut cream to loosen it up if necessary. Set aside.

Once the biscuits are firm, spread a thin layer of jam over half the biscuits leaving a slight gap around the edges. Return to the freezer for 10–15 minutes for the jam to set.

Once the jam has set, dollop a spoonful of the marshmallow mixture on top of the jam-covered biscuits, leaving a gap around the edges as before, then top with the remaining biscuits and gently press down to sandwich everything together. Return to the freezer for 1 hour.

For the chocolate coating, melt the chocolate in a small saucepan over low heat, stirring, until thick and creamy.

It's dipping time! Press a bamboo skewer through one of the biscuit sandwiches to hold everything together, then dip it into the melted chocolate to coat completely. Return the wagon wheel to the tray and repeat with the remaining biscuit sandwiches, then place the tray in the fridge for 30 minutes to set. Enjoy straightaway, or keep in an airtight container in the fridge for up to 7 days or in the freezer for up to 3 months.

TIP

This recipe yields more jam than you need here, so store the excess in an airtight container in the fridge for up to 7 days or in the freezer for up to 3 months – it's great spread on your favourite paleo loaf.

'Ferrero Rochers' Ⓛⓒ Ⓢ Ⓥ Ⓡ

MAKES 10–12

Growing up, 'Ferreros' (as my mum would call them) were always reserved for special occasions – if I was really lucky I would get a few stuffed into my stocking at Christmas time. The combo of hazelnuts and chocolate is a real winner, and I defy you not to devour this healthy low-carb version straight after making it!

420 g (3 cups) hazelnuts
90 g (1 cup) desiccated coconut
60 g (½ cup) cacao powder
½ teaspoon stevia
¼ teaspoon sea salt
1 vanilla pod, split and seeds
   scraped, or 1 teaspoon vanilla
   powder
250 g hazelnut or macadamia
   nut butter
2 tablespoons coconut oil
250 g (2 cups) Luke's Dark
   Chocolate (see page 224),
   roughly chopped

Add 280 g (2 cups) of the hazelnuts to a food processor, along with the desiccated coconut, cacao powder, stevia, salt and vanilla and blitz until well combined. Add the nut butter and coconut oil and whiz again to form a thick, wet paste.

Using your hands, take a walnut-sized piece of the mixture and roll it into a rough ball, then press one of the remaining whole hazelnuts into the centre and roll it again between your palms to give the ball a nice smooth surface. Place the ball on a baking tray and repeat with the rest of the mixture, then transfer to the freezer for 20 minutes to chill and firm.

While the balls are chilling, get your dipping and rolling station ready. Roughly chop the remaining hazelnuts and transfer them to a shallow bowl. Melt the chocolate in a small saucepan over low heat, stirring as you go, until thick and creamy.

Using your fingers, dip one of the chilled balls briefly into the chocolate to coat completely, then add to the bowl with the chopped hazelnuts and roll to coat. Place the ball back on the tray and repeat with the rest, then return the tray to the freezer for 5 minutes for the chocolate to set. Keep the chocolate warm over low heat.

Once the first layer of chocolate has had a chance to set, dip the balls back in the chocolate as before, then transfer to the fridge until ready to serve.

THE LOWDOWN

Hazelnuts contain phytochemicals that belong to a group of nutrients called flavonoids, which have been proven to support brain health, improve circulation and reduce symptoms associated with allergies. There you have it – all the permission you need to eat these beauties in abundance!

Blueberry galette ⓢ

SERVES 8-10

A galette is a term used in French cuisine to designate various types of flat, round or freeform crusty cakes. In my eyes they are the pie's quicker and easier little sister, with no fussing needed to make the crust or to make sure everything looks perfect – the whole point of a galette is that it's nice and rustic. I've used blueberries here, but raspberries work really beautifully too.

2 tablespoons coconut sugar, plus extra for sprinkling
2 teaspoons arrowroot or tapioca flour
1 vanilla pod, split and seeds scraped, or 1 teaspoon vanilla powder
300 g (2 cups) fresh blueberries
1 egg, beaten
½ teaspoon ground cinnamon
Whipped Vanilla Coconut Cream (see page 262), to serve (optional)

Crust
155 g (1½ cups) almond meal
65 g (½ cup) arrowroot or tapioca flour
1 vanilla pod, split and seeds scraped, or 1 teaspoon vanilla powder (optional)
1 tablespoon coconut sugar
½ teaspoon sea salt
100 g butter, chilled and cubed
1 egg, chilled

For the crust, add the almond meal, arrowroot or tapioca flour, vanilla, coconut sugar, salt and butter to a food processor and pulse to combine. Add the egg and continue to pulse to form a nice, wet dough. Roll into a ball, wrap in plastic wrap and transfer to the fridge to chill for 30 minutes.

Preheat the oven to 180°C and line a baking tray with baking paper.

Mix the coconut sugar, arrowroot or tapioca flour and vanilla in a bowl. Gently stir in the blueberries to coat.

Remove the chilled dough from the fridge and roll it out between two pieces of baking paper into a circle approximately 25 cm in diameter. Transfer the pastry to the prepared baking tray, then spoon the blueberry mixture into the centre, leaving a 5 cm border around the edge.

Lifting up the edges of your baking paper to give you leverage, carefully fold over the edges of the pastry towards the centre and up to the filling, pressing the folded dough with your fingers as you go to hold it together.

Brush the folded pastry border with the beaten egg and sprinkle it with 1 teaspoon of extra coconut sugar and the cinnamon. Transfer the galette to the oven and bake for 30 minutes, or until the blueberries are soft and the crust is golden brown and crispy.

Remove from the oven and leave to cool slightly, then cut into slices and serve with whipped vanilla coconut cream, if you like. Any leftovers can be stored in an airtight container in the fridge for up to 4 days.

Peanut butter nice-cream cake

SERVES 10-12

I'm not sure if I could have combined two of my favourite things more gloriously! Easy homemade nice cream (that's right, no churners here – ain't nobody got time for that!) and peanut butter, because... well, that's obvious. Whether you're celebrating a birthday or just the fact that you made it to 5 pm in one piece, this is one recipe that you will adore.

300 g (3 cups) walnuts or pecans, roughly chopped
90 g (1 cup) desiccated coconut
3 tablespoons cacao powder
2 tablespoons coconut oil or butter, softened

Caramel sauce
150 g butter
3 tablespoons honey or pure maple syrup
125 ml (½ cup) coconut cream

Nice cream
620 g (4 cups) cashew nuts, soaked in water for 3 hours, drained
2 avocados
375 ml (1½ cups) coconut cream
500 g (2 cups) unsalted smooth peanut butter
60 g (½ cup) cacao powder
1 teaspoon sea salt
½ teaspoon stevia
1 teaspoon ground cinnamon

To serve (optional)
125 g (1 cup) Luke's Dark Chocolate (see page 224), melted
2 tablespoons roughly chopped toasted peanuts

Line the base and sides of a 23 cm springform cake tin with baking paper.

In a food processor, blitz the walnuts or pecans, desiccated coconut and cacao powder to a fine crumb, then add the oil or butter and blitz again to form a moist crumb-like consistency. Spoon the mixture into the prepared cake tin and use your fingers to press it into the base and side in an even layer to cover completely. Transfer to the freezer and leave for 40 minutes, or until set.

While the crust is setting, make the caramel sauce. Melt the butter and honey or maple syrup in a saucepan over medium heat, stirring to combine. Bring to the boil, then reduce to a simmer and leave to bubble away for 4–5 minutes, until nicely thickened. Remove from the heat and slowly stir in the coconut cream, then transfer to a bowl and set aside to cool.

For the nice cream, place the cashew nuts in the food processor or a high-speed blender with the avocados and coconut cream and pulse until smooth. Add the remaining ingredients and continue to blend until deliciously smooth and creamy.

Remove the tin from the freezer and spoon the nice cream filling over the base and up the side, smoothing the surface with a back of a spoon. Return to the freezer for 30 minutes to set slightly, then pour over the caramel sauce in an even layer and transfer to the freezer for 30 minutes, or until firm.

When ready to eat, remove from the freezer, drizzle with the melted dark chocolate and top with the toasted peanuts, if you like. Cut into wedges with a warm knife and serve.

BASICS

Whipped vanilla coconut cream (LC) (S) (V) (NF) (R)

MAKES ABOUT 375 ML (1½ CUPS)

1 x 400 ml can coconut cream,
   refrigerated upside down
1 tablespoon pure maple syrup
1 teaspoon vanilla extract

Scoop the solid set coconut cream from the can into a bowl, being careful not to add any of the clear coconut liquid (keep this for using in smoothies, sauces and curries). Add the maple syrup and vanilla extract to the cream, then use a hand-held blender on high speed to whisk until thick and well combined.

Store in an airtight container in the fridge for up to 5 days. Try it spooned on top of your breakfast, dolloped into a hot drink or served alongside your favourite dessert.

Cauliflower rice (K) (LC) (S) (V) (NF)

MAKES ABOUT 800 G (4 CUPS)

1 head of cauliflower, florets and
   stalk roughly chopped
2 tablespoons coconut oil
sea salt

Place the chopped cauliflower in a food processor and pulse into tiny rice-like pieces. This usually takes six to eight pulses. Melt the coconut oil in a large frying pan over medium heat, add the cauliflower rice and saute for 4–6 minutes, or until softened. Season with salt to taste.

Mayo (K) (LC) (S) (NF) (R)

MAKES ABOUT 300 ML

1 egg yolk, at room temperature
1 tablespoon lemon juice
½ teaspoon sea salt
250 ml (1 cup) extra-virgin olive oil

Place the egg yolk, lemon and salt in a food processor and blend for 20 seconds or so to combine. With the motor running, add the oil in a slow, steady stream until all the oil has been incorporated and the mayo is thick and creamy.

Store in an airtight container in the fridge for up to 5 days.

FURTHER READING

Body composition

Learn more about the benefits of building lean muscle mass and reducing body fat (mentioned on page 11).

B. Strasser et al., 'Role of dietary protein and muscular fitness on longevity and aging', *Aging and Disease*, 2018, vol. 9, no. 1, pp. 119–32.

C. Castaneda et al., 'Elderly women accommodate to a low-protein diet with losses of body cell mass, muscle function, and immune response', *American Journal of Clinical Nutrition*, 1995, vol. 62, no. 1, pp. 30–39.

D.W. Haslam & W.P. James, 'Obesity', *Lancet*, 2005, vol. 366., no. 9492, pp. 1197–209.

Carbohydrates

Find out more about human history and carbohydrate consumption (mentioned on page 25).

Cordain, et al 2000 Am J of Clinical Nutrition & 2 S.B. Eaton Proceedings of the Nutrition Society, 2006, 65, 1-6.

Price, Weston, DDS, *Nutrition and Physical Degeneration*, 1945, Price-Pottenger Nutrition Foundation, San Diego, CA, 59-72.

Fat

Learn more about why fat is your brain's best friend (mentioned on page 10).

M.F. Muldoon et al., 'Long-chain omega-3 fatty acids and optimization of cognitive performance', *Military Medicine*, 2014, vol. 179, suppl. 11, pp. 95–105.

Find out more about the benefits of eating butter from grass-fed cows (mentioned on page 143).

Fallon, S, and Enig, M, *Nourishing Traditions: The Cookbook That Challenges Politically Correct Nutrition and the Diet Dictocrats*, 2003, 2nd edn., pp. 15.

Read about trans fatty acids (mentioned on page 17).

Mei Zhang & Xiao-Jiao Yang, 'Effects of a high fat diet on intestinal microbiota and gastrointestinal diseases, *World Journal of Gastroenterology*, 2016, vol. 22, no. 40, pp. 8905–909.

M.P. Iqbal et al., 'Trans fatty acids – a risk factor for cardiovascular disease', *Pakistan Journal of Medical Sciences*, 2014, vol. 30, no. 1, pp. 194–97.

Glycogen

Discover more about how the body is able to switch its main fuel source from glycogen to fat (mentioned on page 22).

J. Jensen et al., 'The role of skeletal muscle glycogen breakdown for regulation of insulin sensitivity by exercise', *Frontiers in Physiology*, 2011, vol. 2, article no. 112.

Intermittent fasting

Learn more about the benefits of intermittent fasting (mentioned on page 27).

L.K. Heilbronn et al., 'Alternate-day fasting in non-obese subjects: effects on body weight, body composition, and energy metabolism', *Am Journal of Clinical Nutrition*, 2005, vol. 81, no. 1, pp. 69–73.

Ketosis

Read more about ketosis (mentioned on pages 13 and 26).

J.C. Newman et al., 'Ketogenic diet reduces midlife mortality and improves memory in aging mice', *Cell Metabolism*, 2017, vol. 26, no. 3, pp. 547–57.

M.P. Mattson et al., 'Meal frequency and timing in health and disease', *Proceedings of the National Academy of Sciences*, 2014, vol. 111, no. 47, pp. 16647–53.

Learn about how ketosis and fat affect the brain (mentioned on page 26).

K.A. Page et al., 'Medium-chain fatty acids improve cognitive function in intensively treated type 1 diabetic patients and support in vitro synaptic transmission during acute hypoglycemia', *Diabetes*, 2009, vol. 58, pp. 1237–44.

M.A. Reger et al., 'Effects of beta-hydroxybutyrate on cognition in memory-impaired adults', *Neurobiology of Aging*, 2004, vol. 25, no. 3, pp. 311–14.

Lactose and dairy products

Find out more about the effect of lactose on the body (mentioned on page 24).

Fallon, S, and Enig, M, *Nourishing Traditions: The Cookbook That Challenges Politically Correct Nutrition and the Diet Dictocrats*, 2003, 2nd edn., pp. 33.

Preventing disease

Find out more about insulin production and maintaining health (mentioned on page 11).

E. Orgel & S.D. Mittelman, 'The links between insulin resistance, diabetes, and cancer', *Current Diabetes Reports*, 2013, vol. 13, no. 2, pp. 213–22.

Protein

Find out more about how protein keeps you satisfied for longer (mentioned on page 10 and 21).

L. Chambers et al., 'Optimising foods for satiety', *Trends in Food Science and Technology*, 2015, vol. 41, no. 2, pp. 149–60.

W.R. Lemon, 'Dietary protein requirements in athletes', *Journal of Nutritional Biochemistry*, 1997, vol. 8, no. 2, pp. 52–60.

Raw and lightly cooked vegetables

Read more about why it's best to avoid over-cooking vegetables (mentioned on page 43).

Fallon, S, and Enig, M, *Nourishing Traditions: The Cookbook That Challenges Politically Correct Nutrition and the Diet Dictocrats*, 2003, 2nd edn., pp. 46-47.

Zinc

Learn more about how zinc affects the immune system (mentioned on page 20).

A.S. Prasad, 'Zinc in human health: effect of zinc on immune cells', *Molecular Medicine*, 2008, vol. 14, nos 5–6, pp. 353–57.

THANK YOU!

First off, a huge thanks to you – yes you! – for continuing to love what I do. It wouldn't be possible for me to share my passion for real food unless I had your incredible support in the kitchen, so thank you for picking up this book and cooking my creations. Keep up the great work looking after yourself, and know that it is very much appreciated.

The entire Pan Macmillan and Plum team deserve the biggest hug each and every time I get to bring out a new book – and I am talking one huge collective group hug of awesomeness – because everyone who brings this together is awesome. I may be highlighting a few names below but without all of you, none of this would be possible, so this is a huge thanks to those not always seen or heard. I hear you and see you even if we have never met, and I am grateful for everything you do.

Mary Small, you truly guided the direction of this book in a way that was so necessary and timely. Your knowledge and intuition in steering me down the path that has resulted in *Smart Carbs* was nothing short of a masterstroke. It has been my most enjoyable book to bring to life, from writing to publication, in every way. Thank you for continuing to believe in me as an author, for seeing what I don't always look for, and for sharing so wisely everything you bring to the table to help books truly reflect their authors.

Lucy Heaver, as this was our second book together, I knew it would be even smoother sailing than before – and I was right. Your ease and patience in all the different stages of bringing this book together has made it a complete joy and pleasure. I am so proud of what we have achieved and I hope you know what a key component you have been in making this book as incredible as I think it is!

Now, how best to sum up the creative dream team? I need to come up with a name for the three incredible individuals who have been with me since day one at Plum. Let's just call them the superstars. Mark Roper, my photographer; Lee Blaylock, my food and props stylist; and Emma Warren, my chef extraordinaire. I didn't think they could exceed the epic-ness that they created for *Eat Clean* and *Healthy Made Easy*, but amazingly, with *Smart Carbs*, they have been able to take it to the next level. They get me. They really do. How I cook, how I'd serve it, and the energy of each and every photo to sum up who I am as a cook. Thank you guys.

Rachael Lane, I am still loving all the little kitchen tips and tricks you showed me during the shoot. You were just the most supportive and helpful person to have on set in Melbourne – thanks for being so on the ball and guiding me at times when I was needing your expertise.

Such a pleasure to work with you again, Jane Winning. How fortunate I am to work with you across this book, having experienced such joy when we did *Eat Clean* together. For me it's so important for people to know that I don't just write the recipes, take some photos and then the book hits shelves. I love when people hear about who actually joins the dots to make it happen from day one right up to completion, and you are integral to this, so thank you.

Can I please request that Ashley Carr attends all shoot days for the next book please? Positive, supportive, uplifting and all-round awesome human. I know how busy you are, but your calm and collective way of getting things done is the biggest help – you're a great soul.

Kirby Armstrong, if I had your eyes and talent I would try to bottle it and sell it and become a rich man. You are an incredible designer, and I can't thank you enough for spending the time and investing the love to represent who I am on each and every page with your skill and finesse.

Simon Davis you're an absolute joy to work with. Thank you for being the best editor I could ask for and putting up with my various versions of cups, grams, centimetres and inches. Couldn't do it without you buddy.

And if it wasn't for the genius work and amazingness of Charlotte Ree and the entire PR team, this book would never be possible. Please never change – you are so good at what you do.

To my nearest and dearest loved ones. Thank you so much for dealing with me during deadlines, tasting the recipes that don't make it into the book for good reason, and backing me up if I doubt myself. You are my backbone and the reason I can keep going every day, because you support and believe in me unconditionally – thank you.

KETO AND LOW-CARB RECIPE INDEX

*Recipes marked with an asterisk can easily be made Keto or Low-Carb by following the suggested substitutions on the recipe page.

INDEX

A Plum book

First published in 2018 by Pan Macmillan Australia Pty Limited
Level 25, 1 Market Street, Sydney, NSW, Australia 2000
Level 3, 112 Wellington Parade, East Melbourne, Victoria, Australia 3002

Design by Kirby Armstrong
Typesetting by Pauline Haas
Editing by Simon Davis
Index by Helena Holmgren
Photography by Mark Roper
Food styling by Lee Blaylock
Food preparation by Emma Warren and Rachael Lane
Colour reproduction by Splitting Image Colour Studio
Printed and bound in China by Imago Printing International Limited

A CIP catalogue record for this book is available from the National Library of Australia.

10 9 8 7 6 5 4 3 2 1